MUSICIANS INSTITUTE

PRIVATE LESSONS

JAZZ-ROCK TRIAD IMPROVISING for Guitar

50 LICKS AND LESSONS FOR CREATING RED HOT LEAD PHRASES

by Jean Marc Belkadi

ISBN 0-634-00158-2

HAL•LEONARD® CORPORATION
7777 W. BLUEMOUND RD. P.O. BOX 13819 MILWAUKEE, WI 53213

Copyright © 2000 by HAL LEONARD CORPORATION
International Copyright Secured   All Rights Reserved

No part of this publication may be reproduced in any form
or by any means without the prior written permission of the Publisher.

Visit Hal Leonard Online at
www.halleonard.com

Table of Contents

Page		CD Track
4	**About this Book**	
4	**About the Audio**	
5	**Introduction**	
6	**Chapter 1: Substitution and Superimposition Techniques in Tonal Music**	
6	Major Key II-V-I Progressions Using Substitution	1-2
6	Major Key II-V-I Progressions Using Superimposition	3-4
7	Minor Key II-V-I Progressions Using Substitution	5-6
8	Minor Key II-V-I Progressions Using Superimposition	7-8
8	Major Key IImi7♭5-V-I Progressions Using Substitution	9-10
9	Major Key IImi7♭5-V-I Progressions Using Superimposition	11-12
9	Major Key II7-V-I Progressions Using Substitution	13-14
10	Major Key II7-V-I Progressions Using Superimposition	15-16
11	**Chapter 2: Open Triad Techniques in Tonal Music**	
11	Major Key II-V-I Progression Using Open Triads	17
11	Minor Key II-V-I Progression Using Open Triads	18
11	Major Key IImi7♭5-V-I Progression Using Open Triads	19
11	Major Key II7-V-I Progression Using Open Triads	20
12	**Chapter 3: Substitution and Superimposition Techniques in Modal Music**	
12	Ma7 Chord Examples	21-24
13	Ma7♯11 Chord Examples	25-28
14	Mi7 Chord Examples	29-32
15	Mi(ma7) Chord Examples	33-36
16	Dominant7 Chord Examples	37-40
18	**Chapter 4: Open Triad Techniques in Modal Music**	
18	Ma7 Chord Examples	41-42
18	Mi7 Chord Examples	43-44
19	Mi(ma7) Chord Examples	45-46
20	Mi6 Chord Examples	47-48
20	Dominant7 and Altered Dominant7 Chord Examples	49-50
21	**Acknowledgments**	
21	**About the Author**	
22	**Guitar Notation Legend**	

Note: Use Track 51 to tune up.

Introduction

In contemporary music, the use of triads is an important element in improvisation and composition. They are as prevalent as scales, modes, arpeggios, rhythms, and intervallic ideas. Like scales and modes, triads can be substituted in tonal and modal music. They can also be superimposed, creating bitonality or polytonality. Superimposed triads give us synthetic scales such as hexatonic (6 note scales = 2 triads), or nonatonic scales (9 note scales = 3 triads).

What Is a Triad?

A triad is a three-note chord made up of a root, third, and fifth. There are four triad families:

Major triad: 1–3–5
Minor triad: 1–♭3–5
Diminished triad: 1–♭3–♭5
Augmented triad: 1–3–♯5

Of course, in everyday applications triads are played with different inversions:

Root position　　　　**Inversion possibilities**
1–3–5　　　　　　　　　3–5–1, 5–1–3, 3–1–5, etc.

Sometimes triads are played with one degree dispersed an octave higher:

regular triads　　　　*open triads*

1　3　5　　　1　5　3

This dispersement procedure creates what is referred to as an open triad, and can be applied to minor, diminished, and augmented triads, as well as major.

Triad Substitution

Triad substitution is where one triad is substituted in place of another. One of the most common is flat-five—or tri-tone substitution. This is when a triad a flat-fifth degree (tri-tone) away is substituted for a chord. For example: instead of playing a G major triad over a G7 chord, a D♭ major triad (D♭ is a flat-fifth away from G) is "substituted."

Triad Superimposition

Triad superimposition is where two or more triads are played one after the other, creating a "dispersed scale" effect of bitonality or polytonality. Of course all triads can be substituted or superimposed in both tonal and modal music, either using the single-note approach or voiced in chord form.

About this Book

The purpose of this book is to help you to create your own ideas using triad concepts. It is divided into two parts: tonal music (II-V-I chord progressions, Chapters 1 and 2) and modal music (Chapters 3 and 4). Keep in mind that the examples do not follow a specific order of difficulty; you can jump in anywhere and work with the licks you like best. You also might want to listen to the CD first to locate the examples that appeal to you the most.

About the Audio

Throughout this book, the numbers in the audio symbols (❶) indicate the CD track number where each example will be found on the accompanying CD.

Each example is played at full tempo, and most are repeated at half speed. In addition, short introductory phrases (which are not transcribed in the examples) are sometimes included to provide a better sense of context and to maintain an improvisational feel.

CHAPTER 1

Substitution and Superimposition Techniques in Tonal Music

Fig. 1 offers an example of tri-tone substitution on the V (G7♭9) chord of a II–V–I progression in the key of C major. Notice that over the G7♭9 harmony, a D♭ major triad is substituted in the second half of the measure.

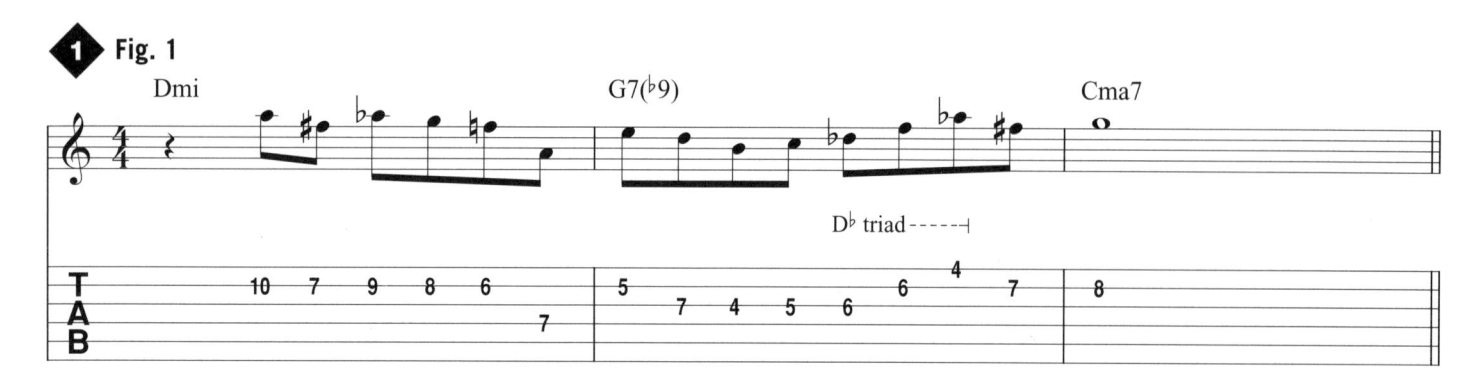

Fig. 1

In Fig. 2 we have triad substitution on the II chord, as well as tri-tone substitution on the V chord. Over the Dmi7 (II) harmony, an E minor triad is substituted. Notice that the connecting note (D) creates a full Emi7 arpeggio.

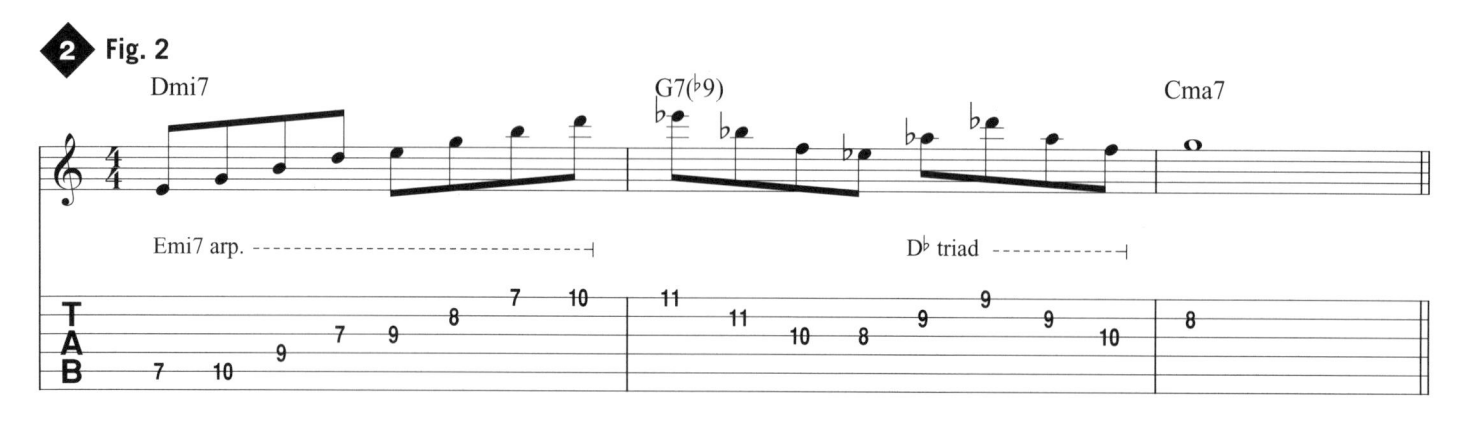

Fig. 2

Fig. 3 is an example of triad superimposition. Over the V chord (A7♭9) we find two substitute triads: the first is an E♭ major triad (tri-tone sub) followed by a D♭ major triad. Notice that the D♭ triad can be seen as a half-step approach to the I chord (Dma7).

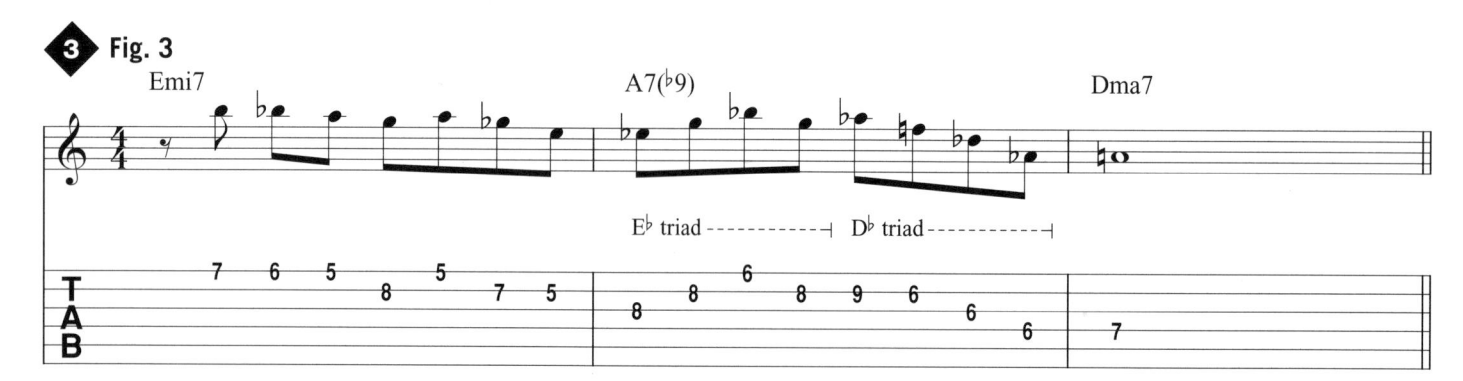

Fig. 3

The next example superimposes two triads over both the II chord (Emi7) and the V chord (A7♭9). In the first measure we have an ascending B augmented triad, followed by a descending A major triad that resolves on the downbeat of the V chord measure. The line continues with a climb up a G major triad, and down a G♭ma7 arpeggio, finally resolving on the fifth degree of the I chord (Dma7).

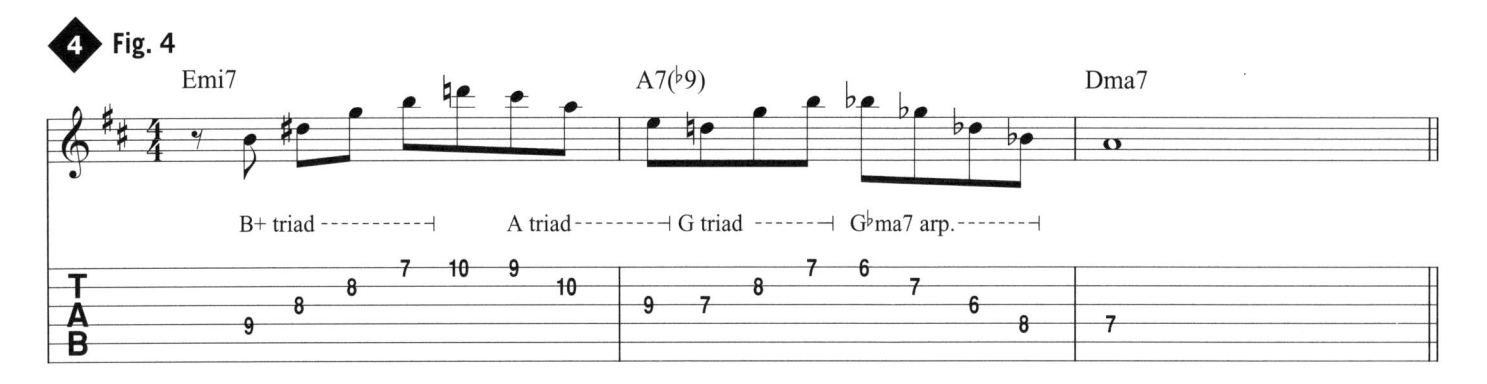

Fig. 4

In this minor II–V–I, a D♭ augmented triad (harmonized from the third degree of the B♭ melodic minor scale) is substituted over the II chord (Gmi7♭5). An E♭ major triad (from the C half-whole diminished scale) is used as a substitution over the V chord (C7♭9).

Fig. 5

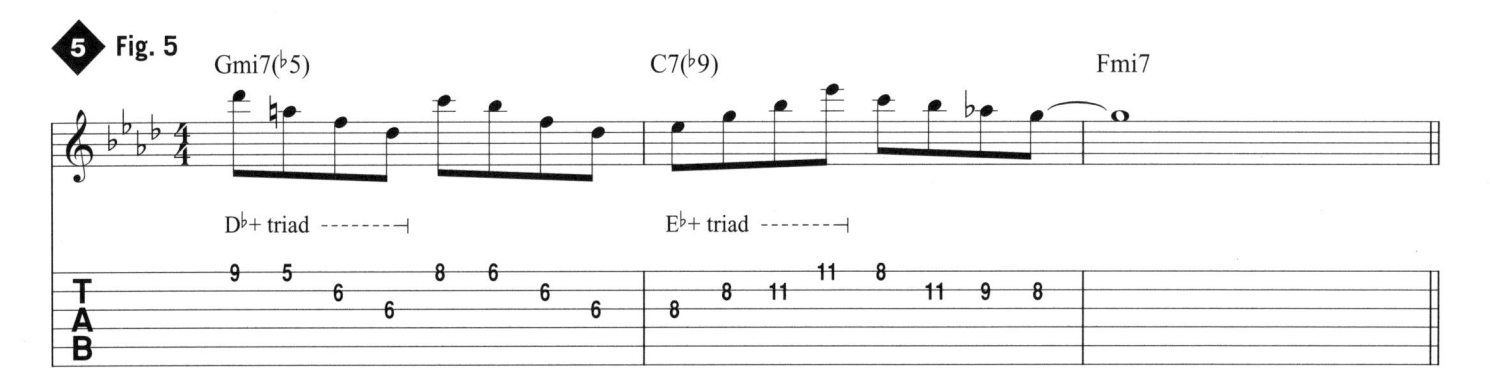

Here's the same progression, but this time the substitution over the II chord is an E♭ triad, from the A♭ major scale. A B♭ minor triad is used over the V chord, illustrating that D♭ major is a useful scale for a C altered chord. (B♭ minor is the relative minor of D♭ major.)

Fig. 6

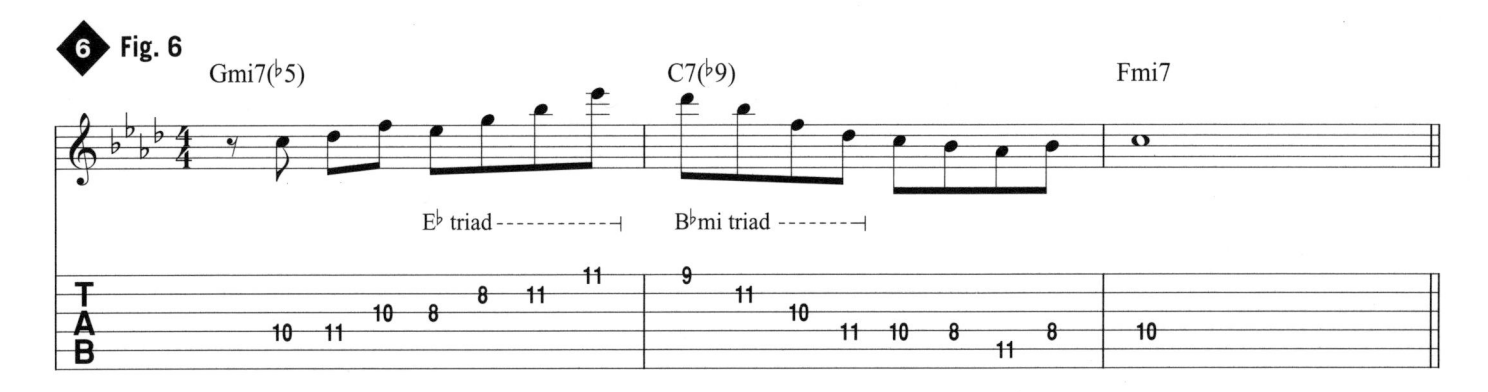

Fig. 7 takes us on a roller coaster ride up and down four superimposed triads (G♭, B♭, A, and B), for a polytonal effect.

Fig. 7

In Fig. 8, Ami7♭5 is once again the departure chord, and Gmi7 is the destination. This time, however, the line takes a "three-steps-forward-and-two-steps-back" motion, as it ascends four superimposed triads and arpeggios—Gma7, D6, E, and B. Be aware that substitution (and the superimposition process) can go beyond triads to 6th, 7th, and extended arpeggios.

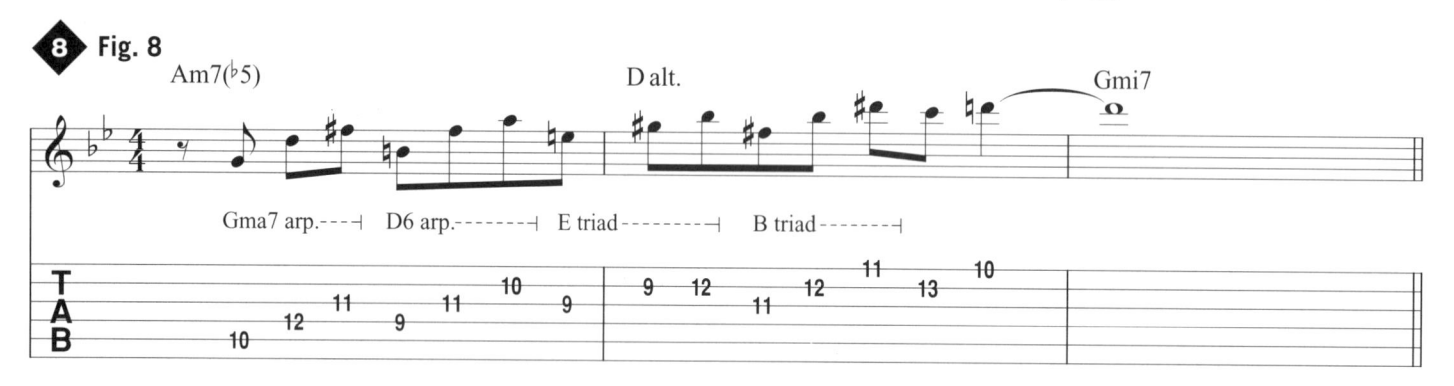

Fig. 8

Here is a IIm7♭5–V–I progression in D major, substituting a D major triad for the II chord (Emi7♭5), and a D♭ma7♯5 arpeggio over the V (A7♭9).

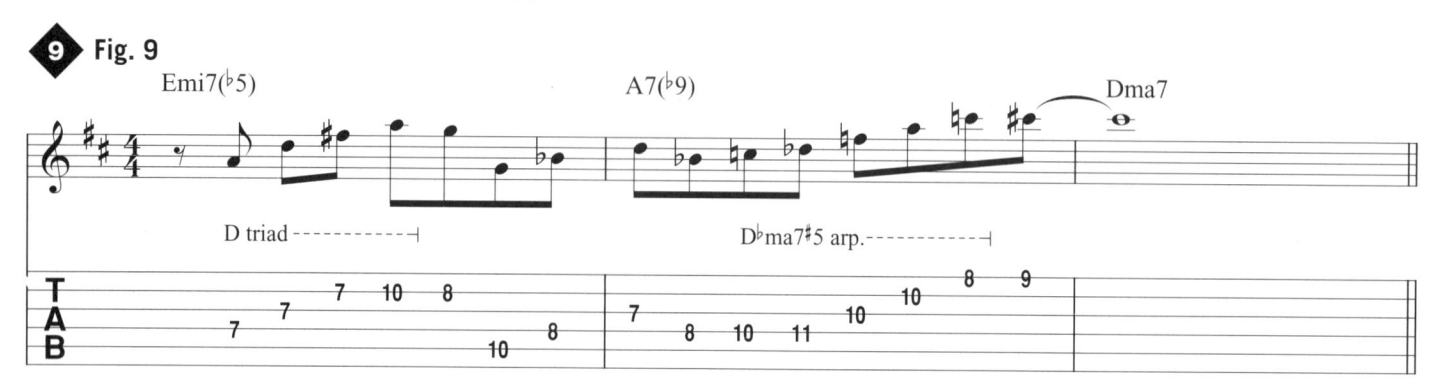

Fig. 9

Here's the same progression again but with a widely dispersed Fma7♯11 arpeggio substitution over the II chord, and a B♭ diminished triad substitution for the V chord.

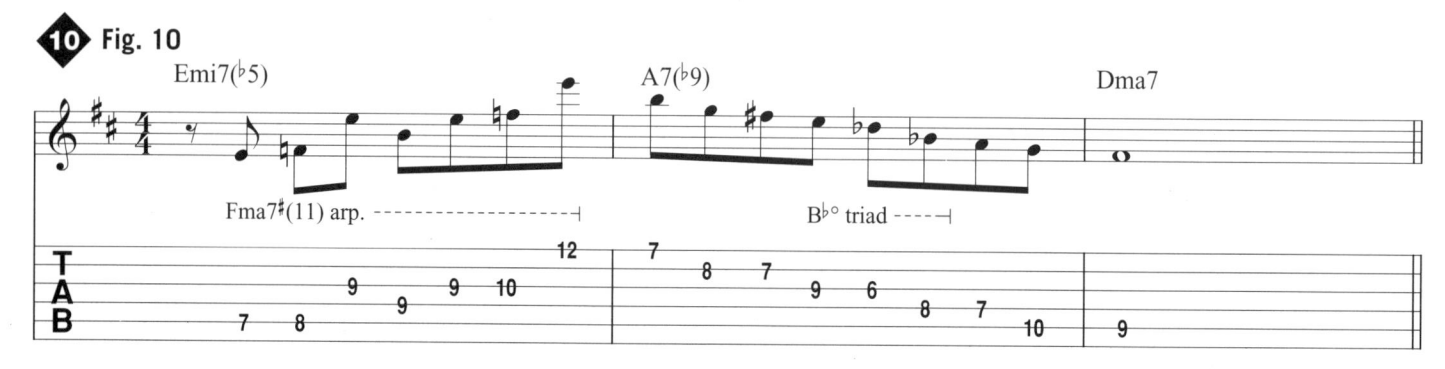

Fig. 10

Fig. 11 uses the same IImi7♭5-V-I progression but in the key of E, and with superimposed triads and arpeggios. Over the II chord (F♯mi7♭5) we have an E major triad and an A6 arpeggio, and over the V chord (B altered) we have Cmaj7♯5 and Ami(ma7) arpeggios.

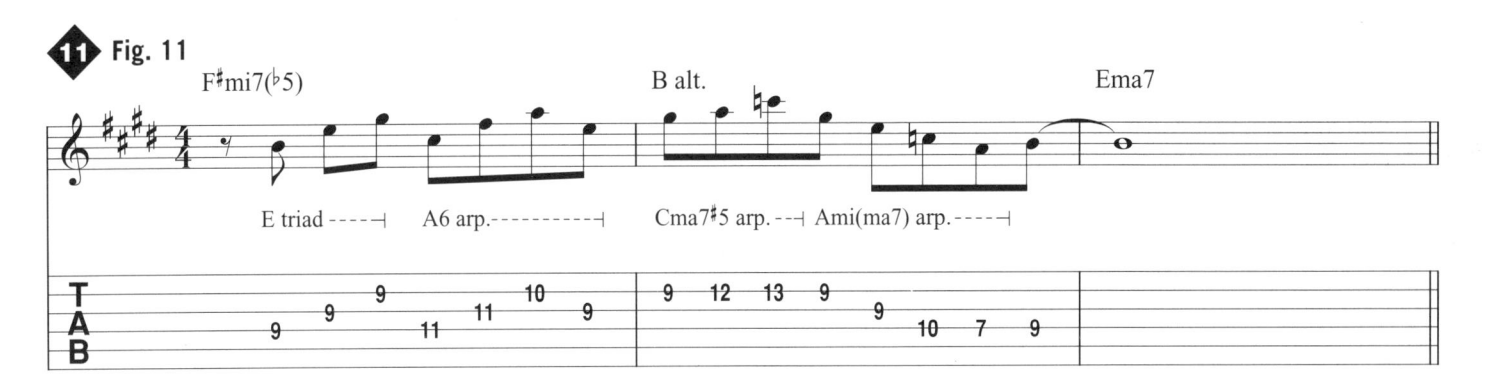

Fig. 11

Fig. 12 superimposes three triads (B, E, and F) over the F♯mi7♭5 chord, and an E major triad over the B altered chord. The resolution notes (A♯ and F♯) imply an E Lydian tonality over the Ema7 chord.

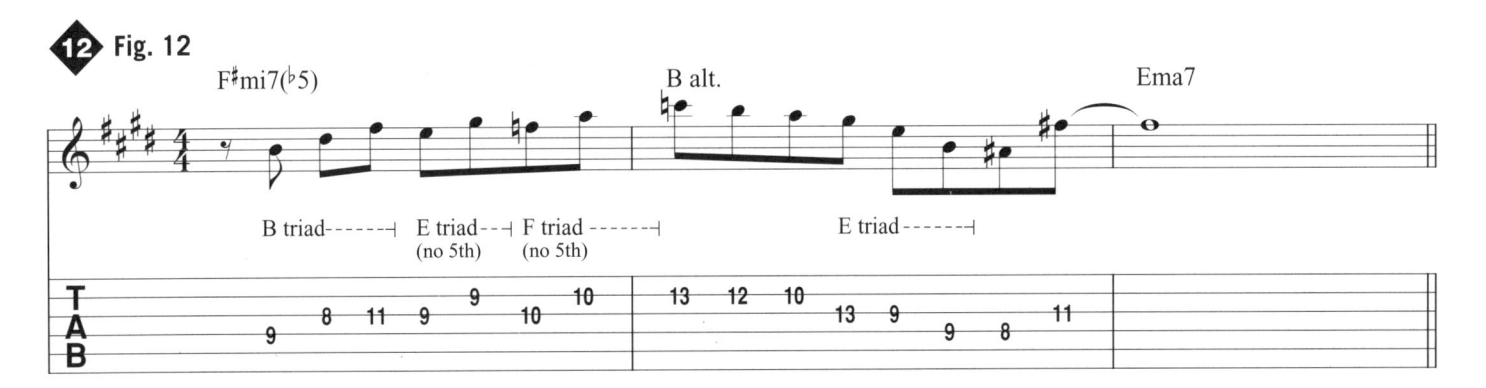

Fig. 12

In this II7–V–I progression, a D♭mi6 arpeggio is substituted over the C7 chord, suggesting the C altered scale. The substitute on the F7♭9 chord is a D major triad, from the F half-whole diminished scale.

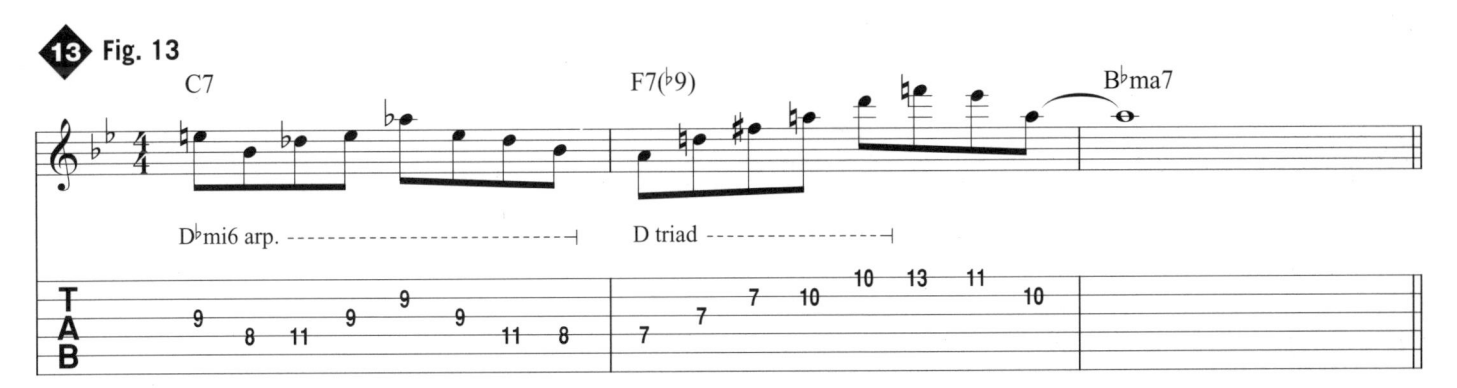

Fig. 13

Here's the same progression but with an ascending A minor, and descending A major triad substitution over the C7 chord. A root position D♭maj7 arpeggio (from F Aeolian) is substituted over the F7♭9 chord.

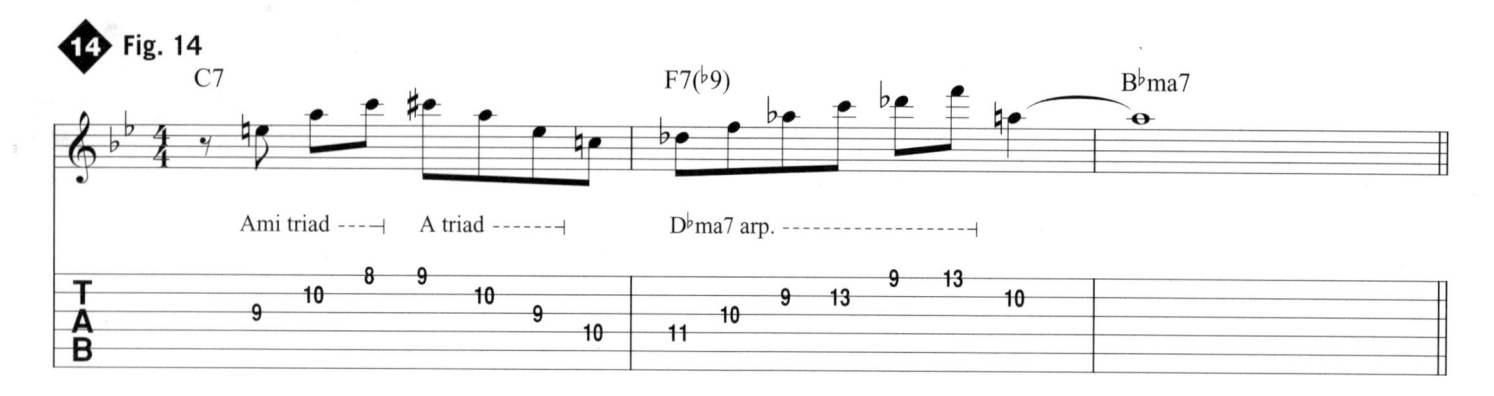

Fig. 14

In Fig. 15, C♯ minor and D major triads are sequenced over the D7 chord, while an A♭ma7 arpeggio substitutes for the G7♭9.

Fig. 15

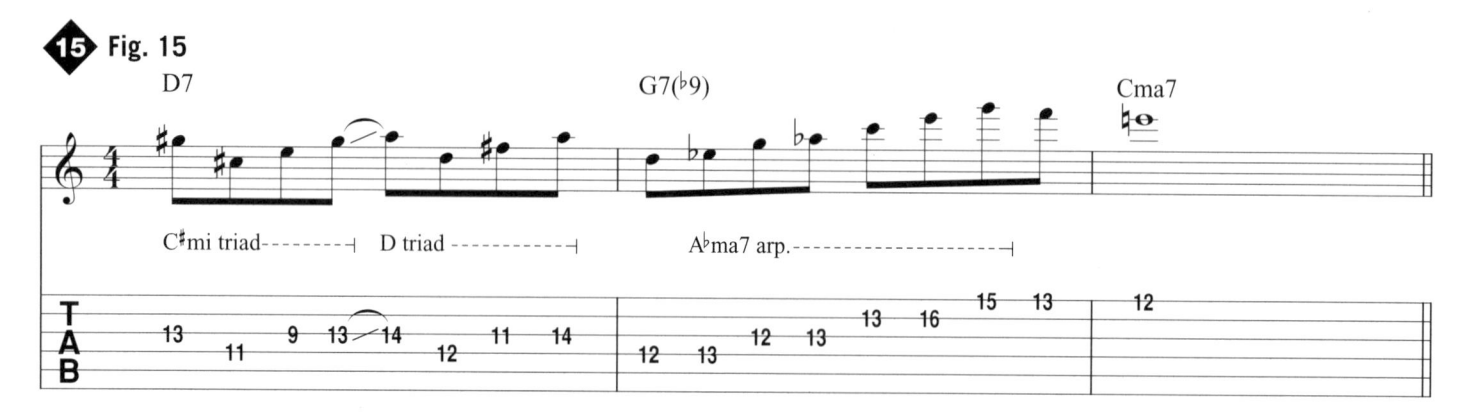

Here's an "out" lick for the same progression. An A♭7 arpeggio is dispersed over the D7 chord, followed by a superimposed F6 arpeggio and B major triad over the G7♭9 chord, resolving to a C Lydian phrase.

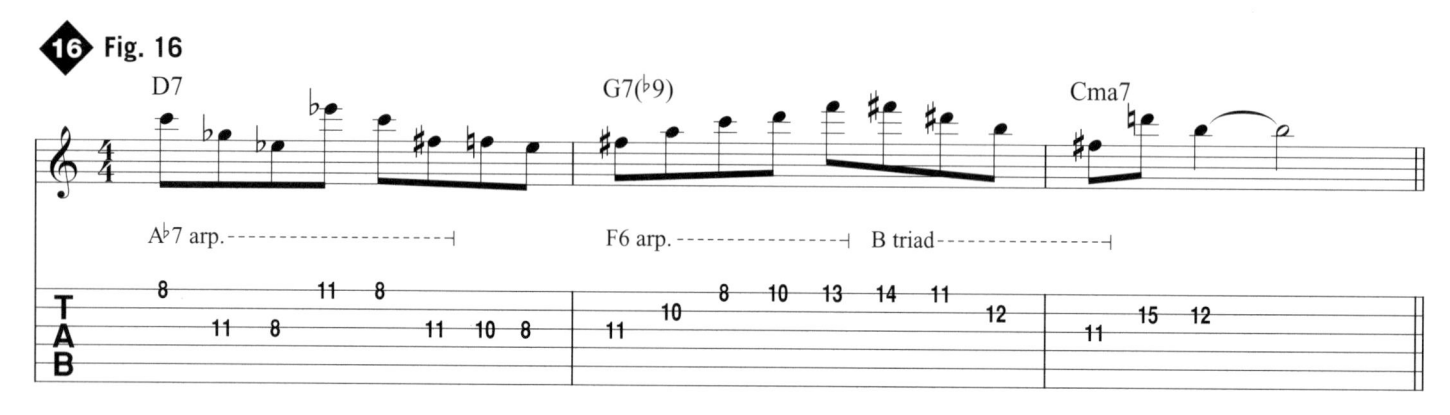

Fig. 16

CHAPTER 2

Open Triad Techniques in Tonal Music

Fig. 17 shows how open triads and arpeggios produce wide intervals for an angular sound. The substitutions are G♭ major triads over the E♭mi7, and a Bdim7 arpeggio over the A♭7 chord.

Fig. 17

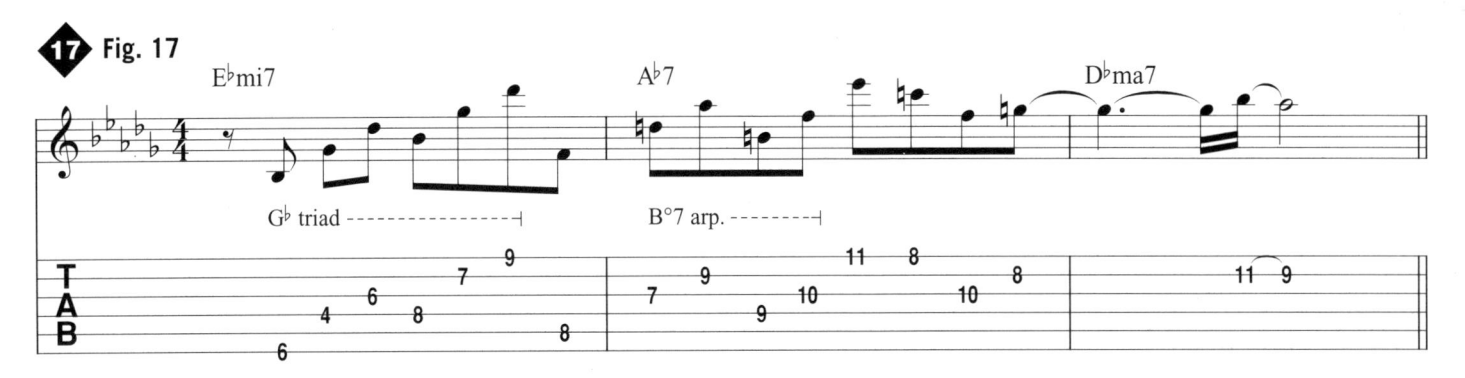

In this II–V–I in E♭ minor, the use of open arpeggios creates a very interesting sound.

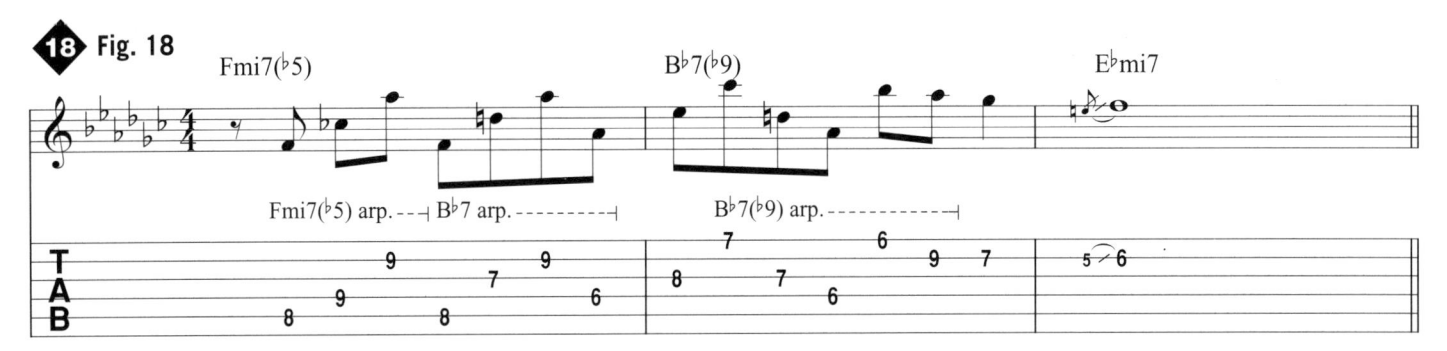

Fig. 18

Fig. 19 substitutes open diminished7 arpeggios over the II chord and resolves with some interesting double-stops.

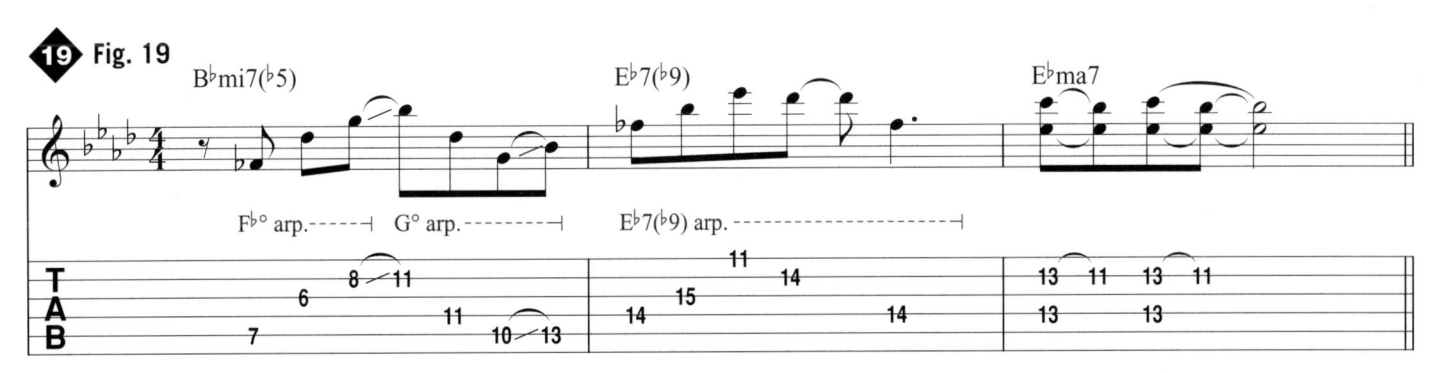

Fig. 19

Open diminished7 arpeggios and a B♭ major triad create wide interval skips in this II7–V–I progression.

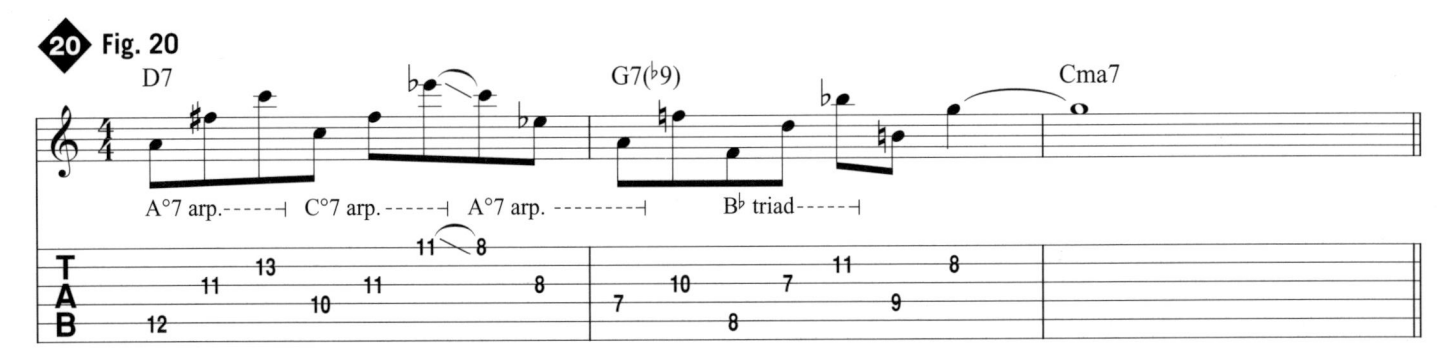

Fig. 20

11

CHAPTER 3

Substitution and Superimposition Techniques in Modal Music

Fig. 21 is a C major progression with a funk/Latin feel. The F#mi7(b5) arpeggio is harmonized from C Lydian and resolves to the proceeding C major line, while the Emi7 arpeggio implies a Cma13 quality.

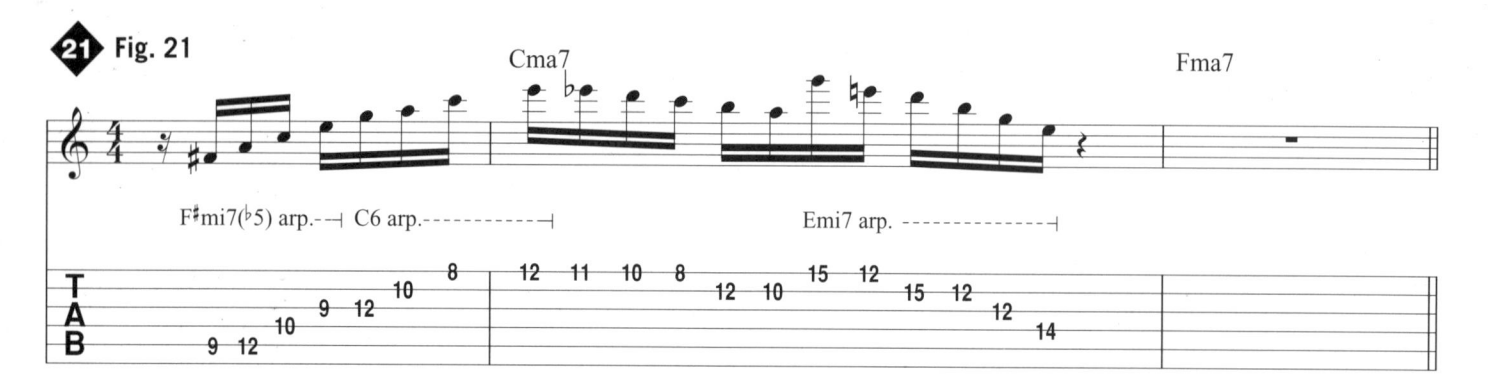

Over the same progression, an A diminished triad supplies a nice, bluesy contrast to the sweet sounding C6 arpeggio and C major triad.

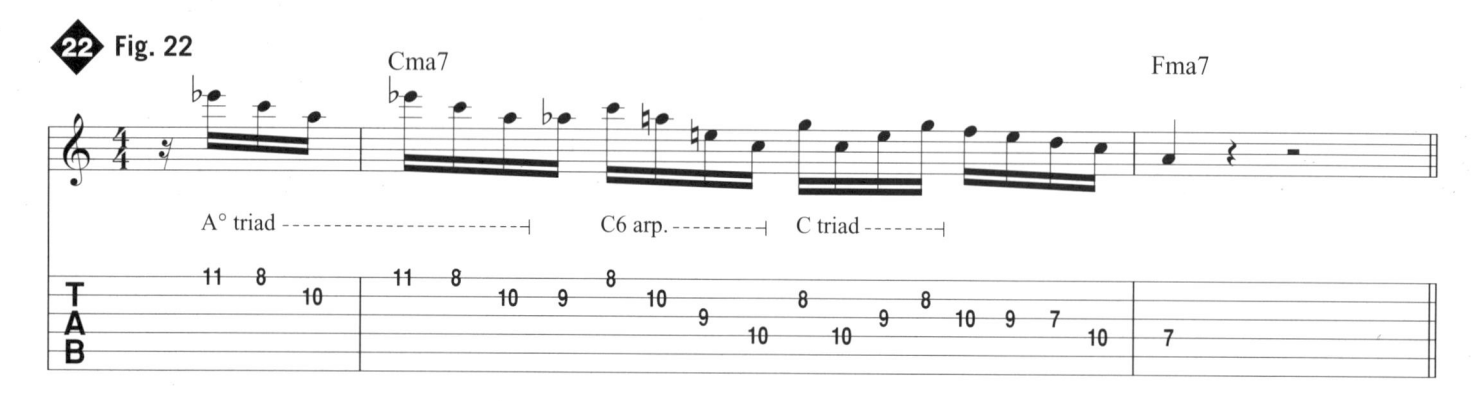

Edim7 arpeggios supply the dissonance in this "outside" lick. Notice how the last two notes resolve on the 3rd and 5th of the Ebma7 chord.

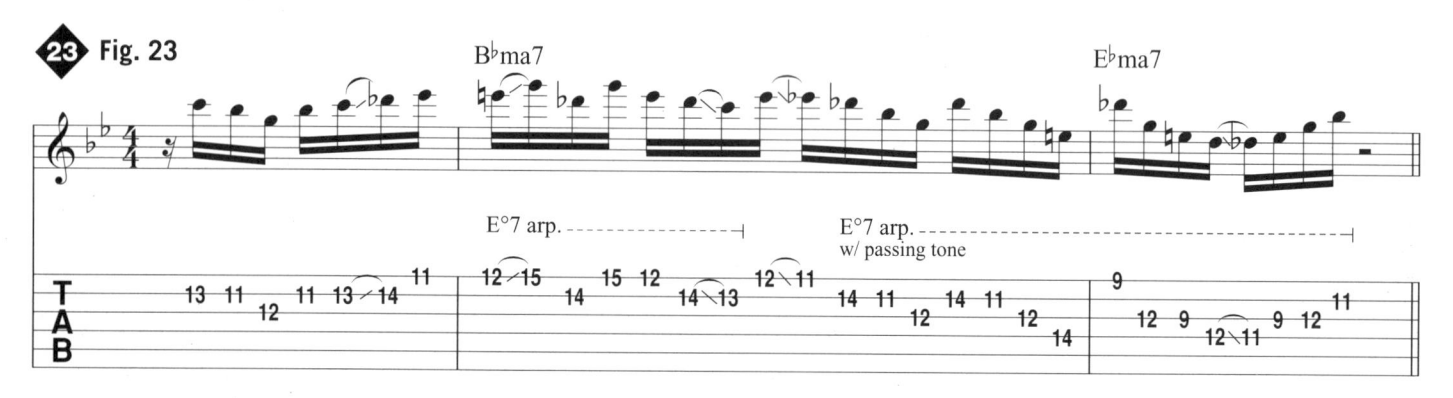

Fig. 24 employs chromatic passing tones to tie together the superimposed G major, E diminished, and B diminished triads.

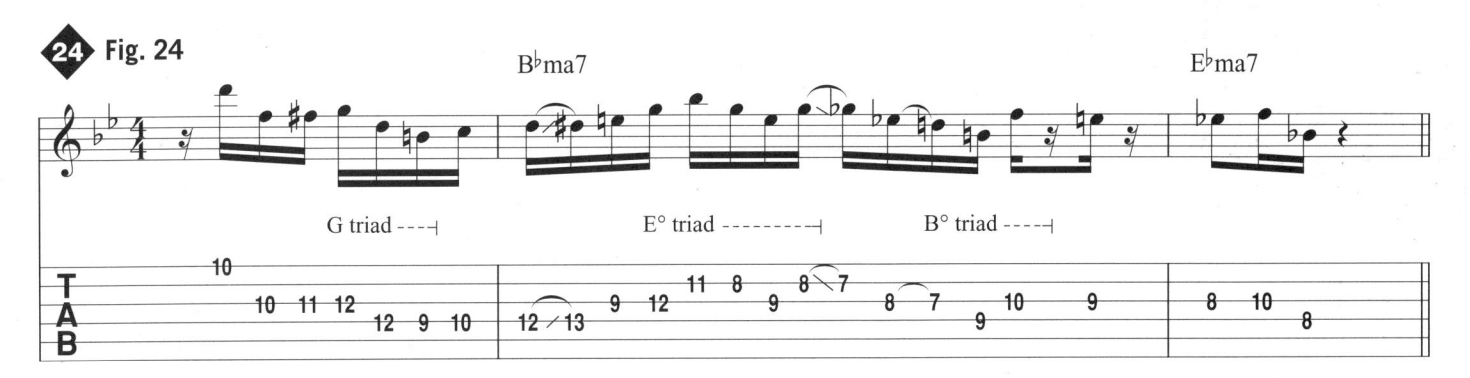

Fig. 24

Here's a tapping lick that spells out F#mi7 and C#mi arpeggios, over a classic A Lydian progression.

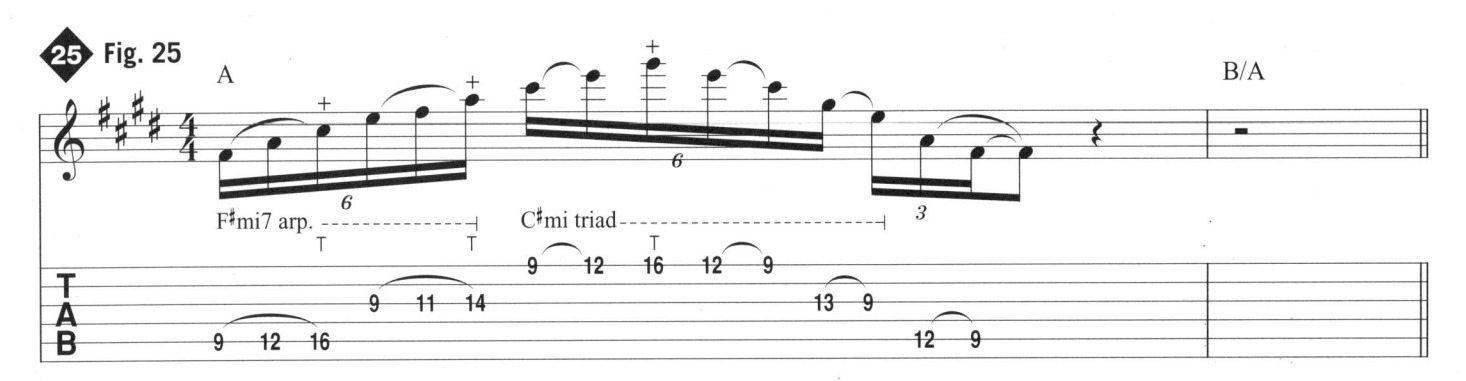

Fig. 25

Here's another tapping lick over the same A Lydian progression that provides a steady stream of triad and arpeggio substitutions.

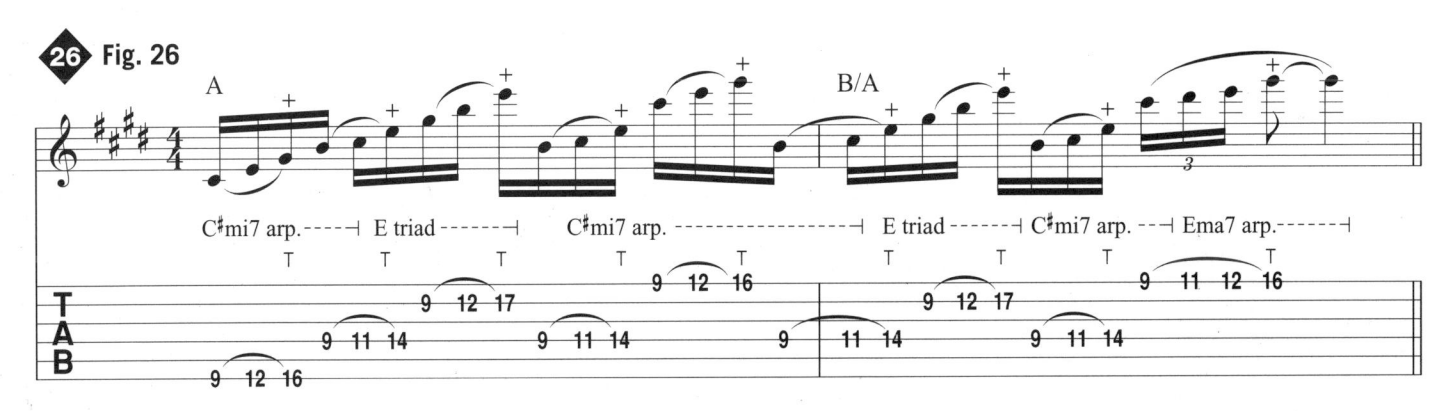

Fig. 26

In this B Lydian progression, F#mi7, D#7, and D9 arpeggios are superimposed.

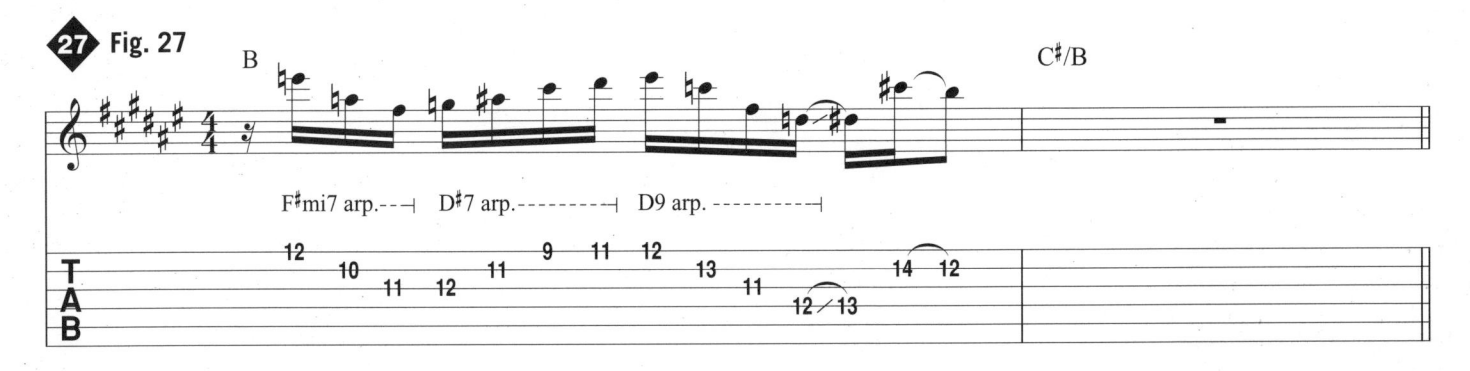

Fig. 27

You won't have to leave 4th position to play the lick in Fig. 28. Following two sequenced patterns, it superimposes three triads (A, B, and D major), and a G#mi7 arpeggio over another B Lydian progression.

Fig. 28

Fig. 29 substitutes a C#mi7♭5 arpeggio over a Dmi7 funk groove, implying a D melodic minor tonality.

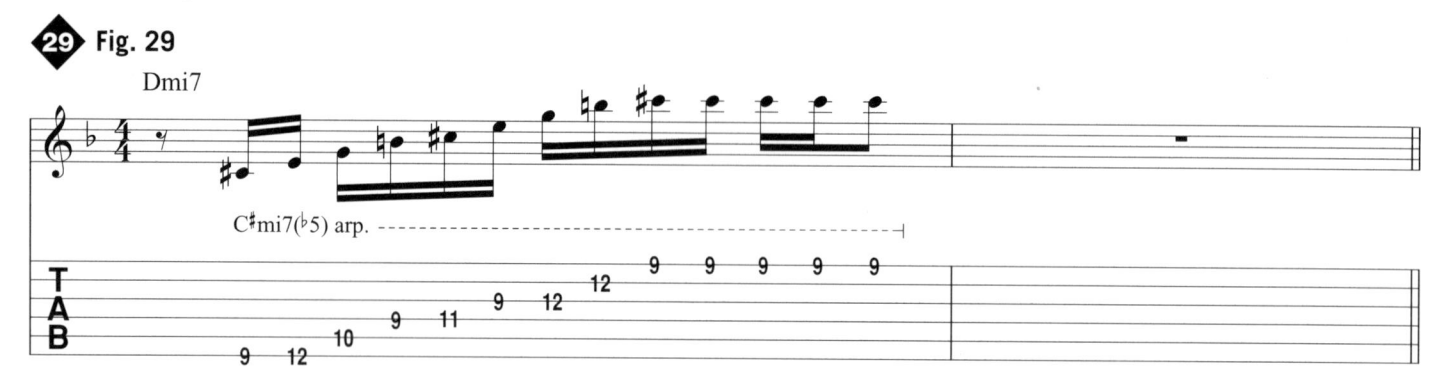

Fig. 29

Here's an example of tri-tone substitution over the same Dmi7 groove. The A♭7 arpeggio (from E♭ melodic minor) supplies some unique, "outside" tones (♭5, ♭9, and major 3rd!) of the Dmi7 chord.

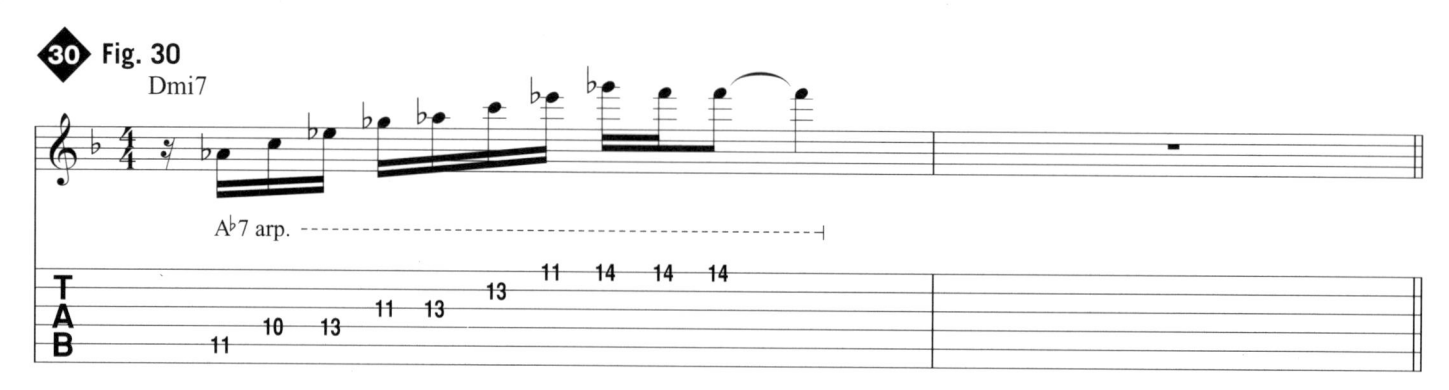

Fig. 30

Fig. 31 combines "inside" substitutions (A♭ major and G minor triads) and "outside" lines for a polytonal effect.

Fig. 31

Here's an F melodic minor lick that superimposes a B♭ triad and a C7 arpeggio (IV and V of F melodic minor) over an Fmi7 chord.

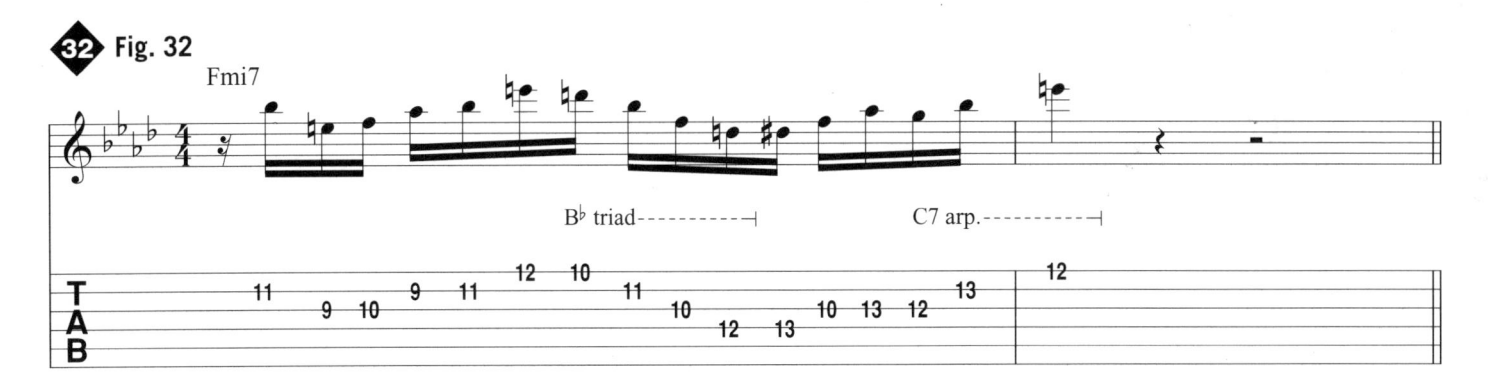

Fig. 32

Over a Bmi(maj7) chord, the substitutions are B diminished and D♭ major triads, harmonized from the B diminished scale.

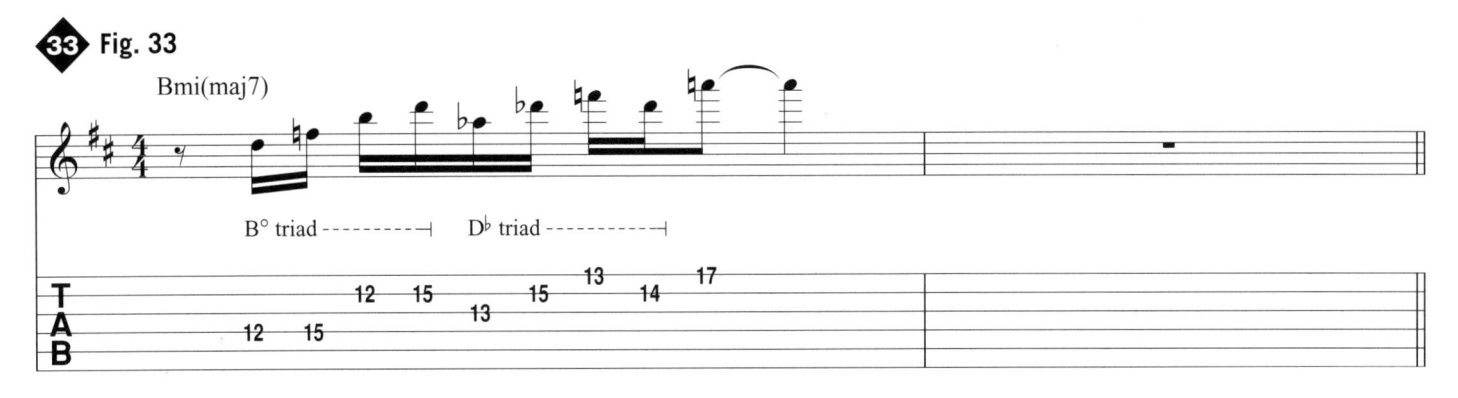

Fig. 33

This Bmi(maj7) lick superimposes F augmented and F♯ augmented triads. Notice that the F♯ augmented is harmonized from B melodic minor.

Fig. 34

Superimposed A minor, and F augmented triads open the door to polytonality in this C♯mi(ma7) example.

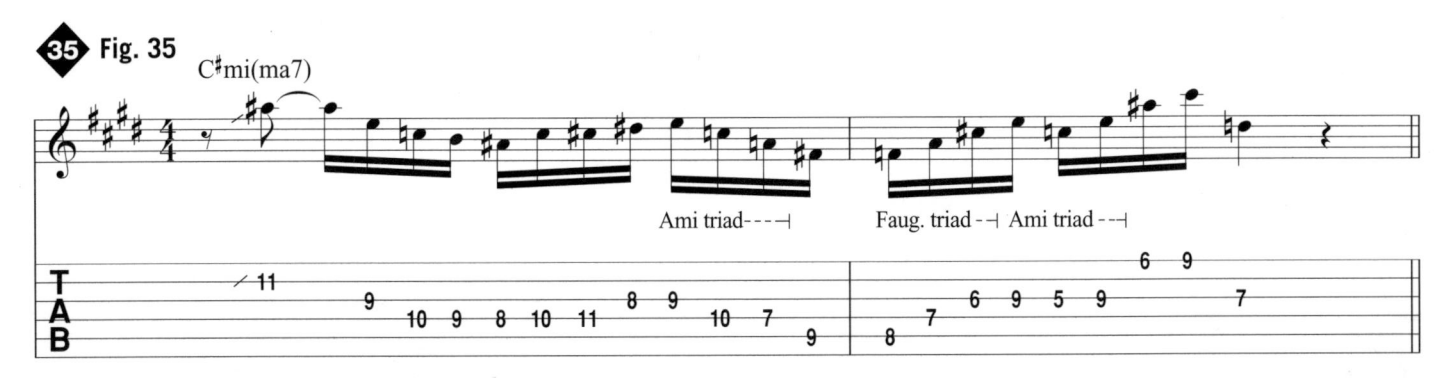

Fig. 35

In Fig. 36 we superimpose an E major triad and a D#7 arpeggio over a C#mi(ma7) chord vamp. As you can see, the superimposition process can be quite complicated, so above all, use your ear.

Fig. 36

An Ami(add9) is the substitute arpeggio in this G Mixolydian lick. Remember to swing the sixteenth notes.

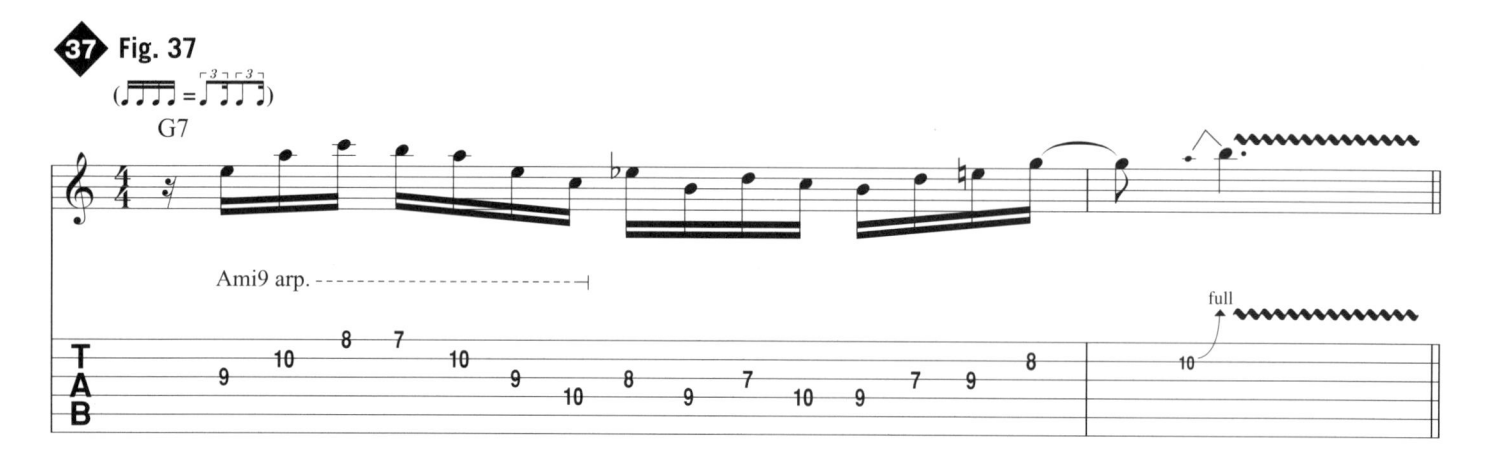

Fig. 37

Here's a sweep-picking lick for a G7 vamp. The E minor triad substitution emphasizes the 13th (E) of the G7 chord.

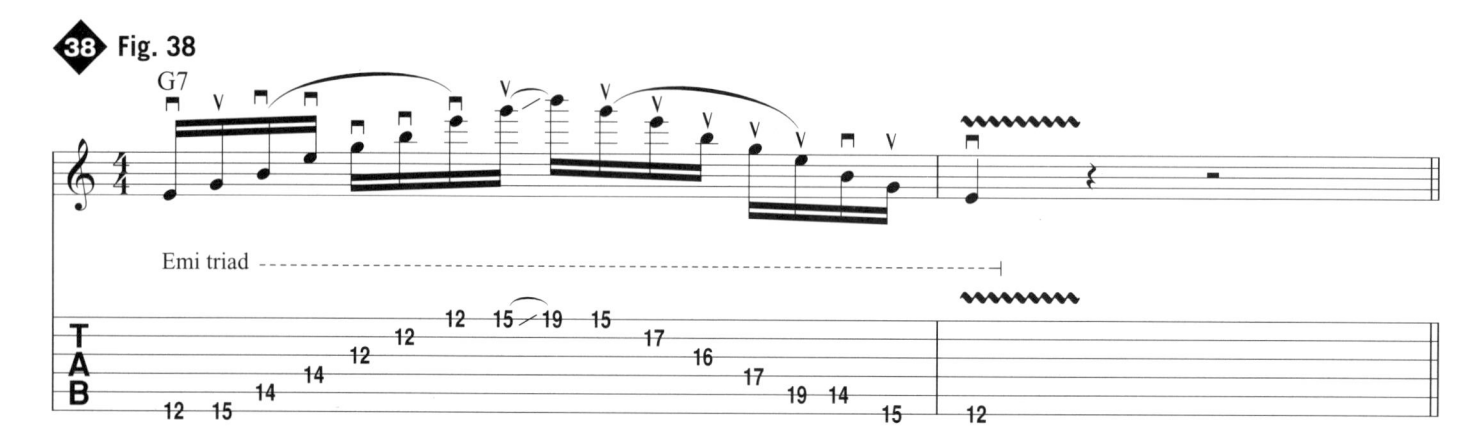

Fig. 38

Superimposed F and G# major triads are lined up with E♭7 and E♭ma7 arpeggios to give this A7 lick an "inside-outside" flavor.

Fig. 39

Fig. 40 gets its minor/major tonality with the help of D major and C augmented superimposed triads, and a resolving A13 arpeggio lick.

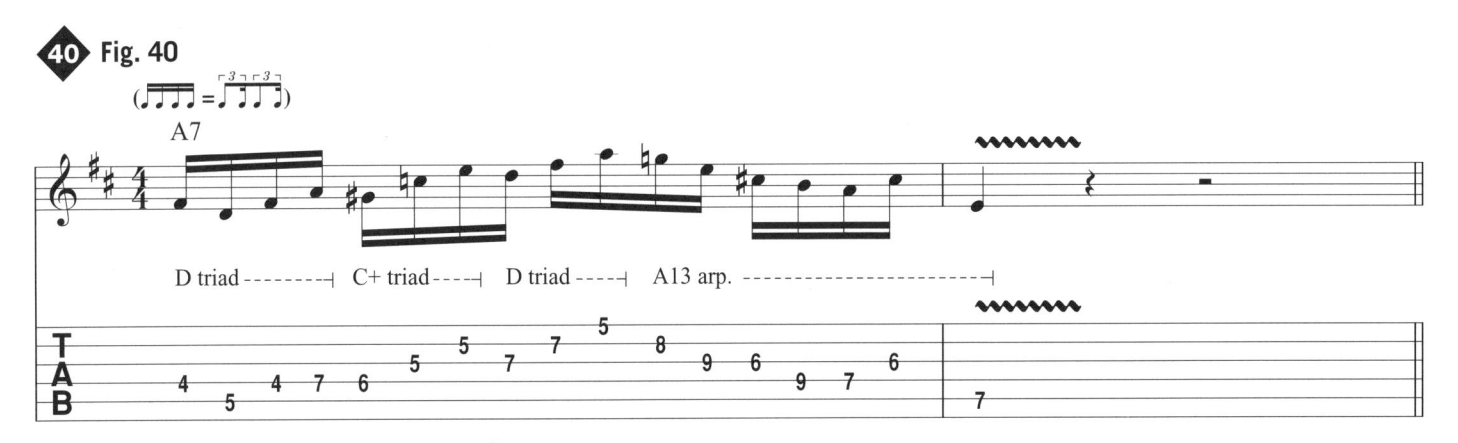

Fig. 40

CHAPTER 4

Open Triad Techniques in Modal Music

Fig. 41 uses a string skipping pattern to substitute three open triads (E minor, C, and G major) over a Cma7 vamp.

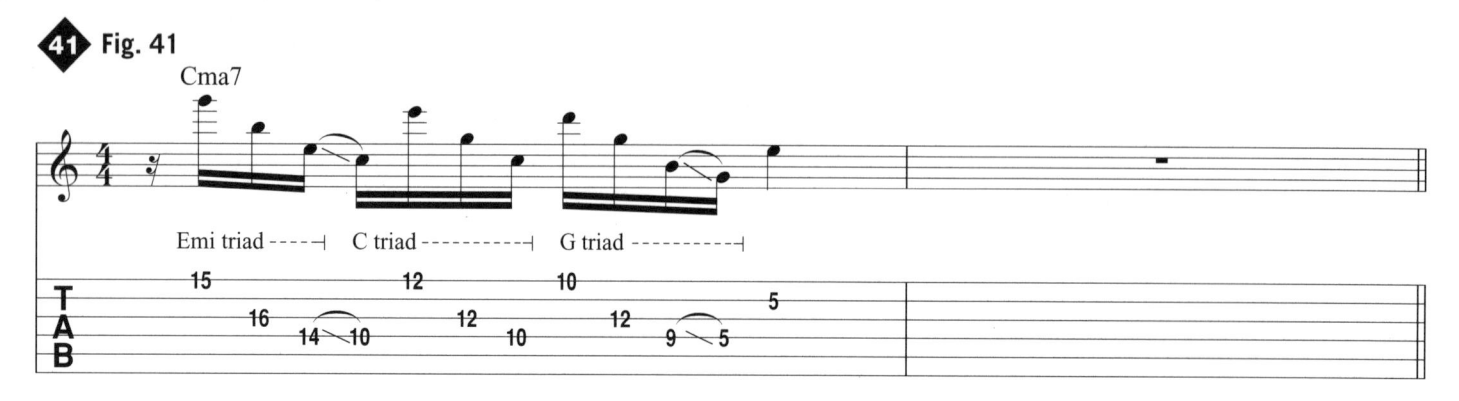

Fig. 41

Here we sequence an open Cma7 arpeggio, and end with a double-stop slide.

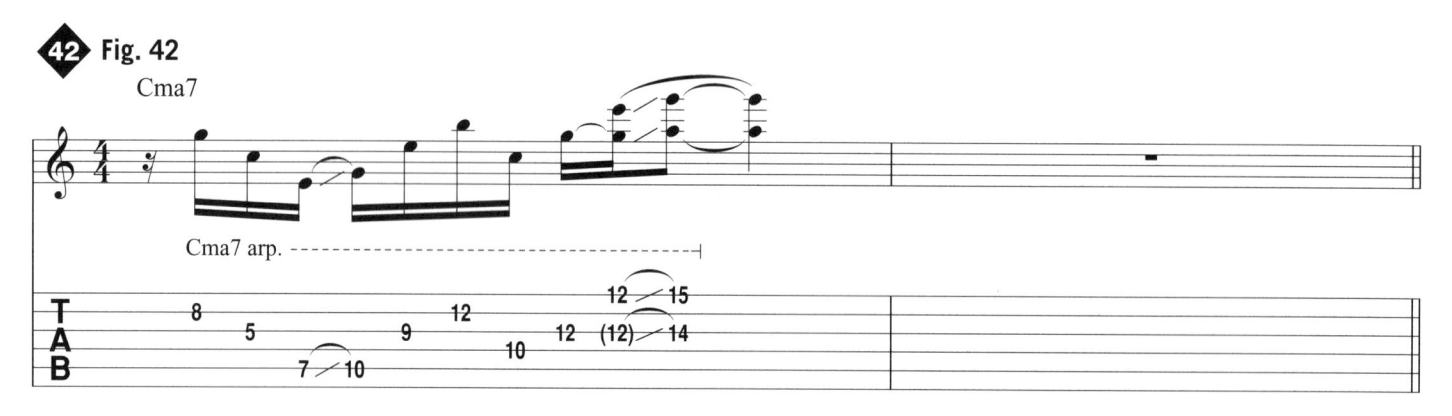

Fig. 42

G minor, A minor, and C major open triads get a workout in this slippery G Dorian lick. Watch out for the slides!

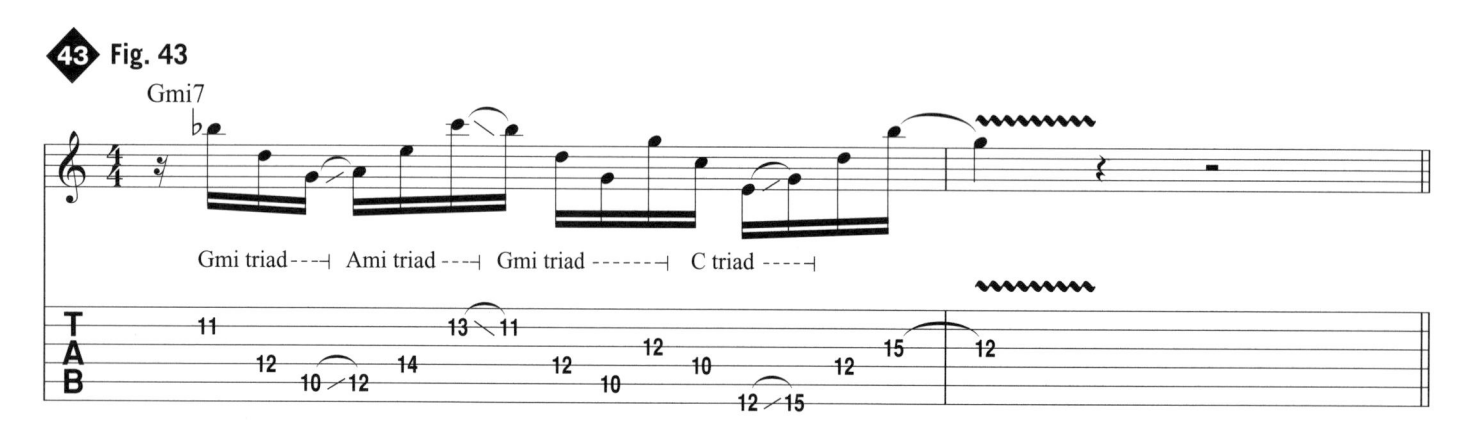

Fig. 43

Fig. 44 is a G Dorian tapping lick that creates a distant, open sound. In the first measure a G minor triad is spread across the top three strings, while in the second, an A minor triad follows in like fashion.

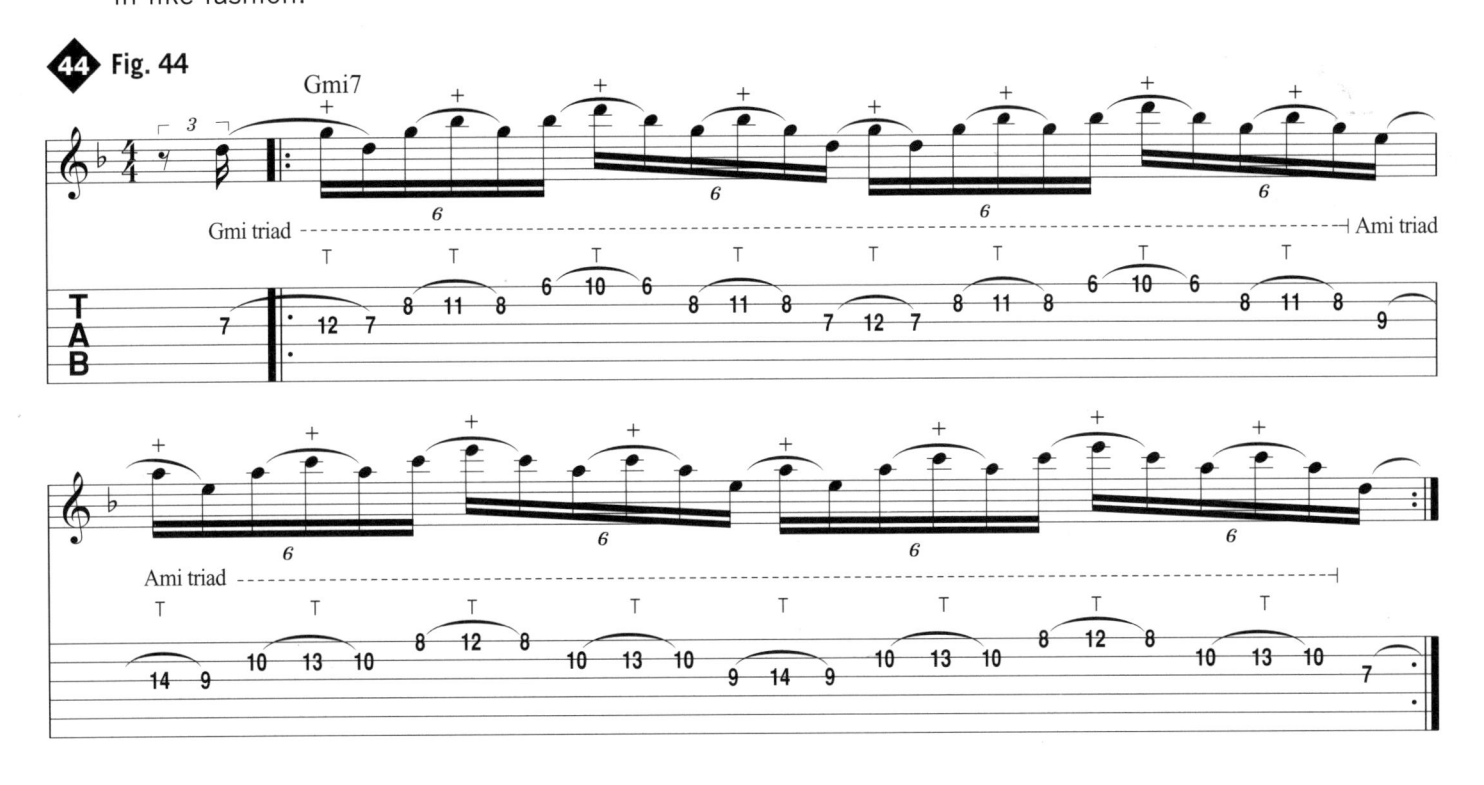

Fig. 44

In this B♭mi(maj7) vamp, we have open B♭mi(ma7) and B♭mi7 arpeggios tied together with a passing, suspended 4th (E♭) degree.

Fig. 45

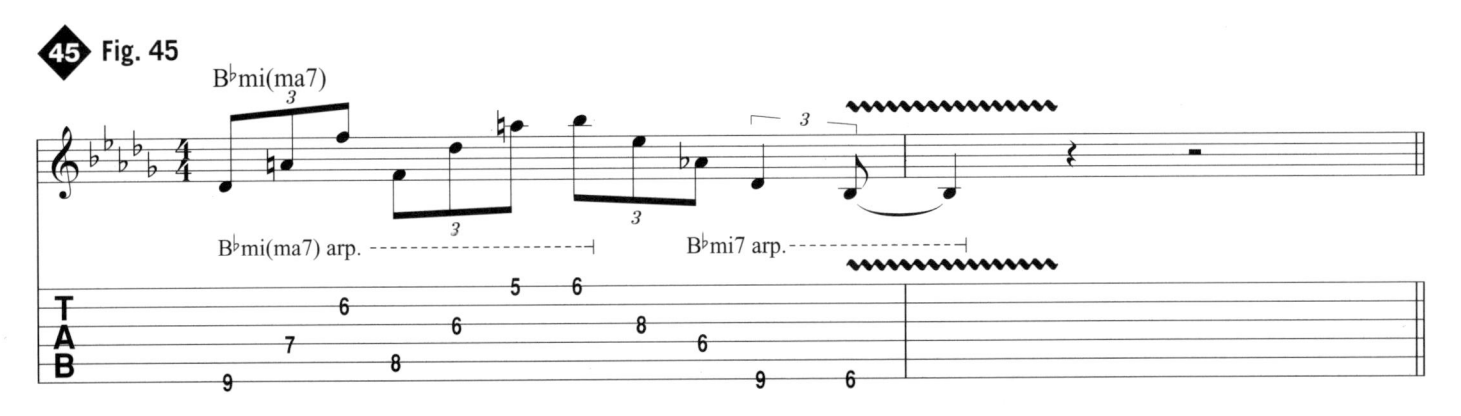

Here's a similar idea, but with an added 9th (C) on the B♭mi7 arpeggio.

Fig. 46

Over a Cmi6 chord, we have three vertical shapes in eighth-note triplet rhythms. The first and third are C minor triads, while the middle one is a Cmi6 arpeggio.

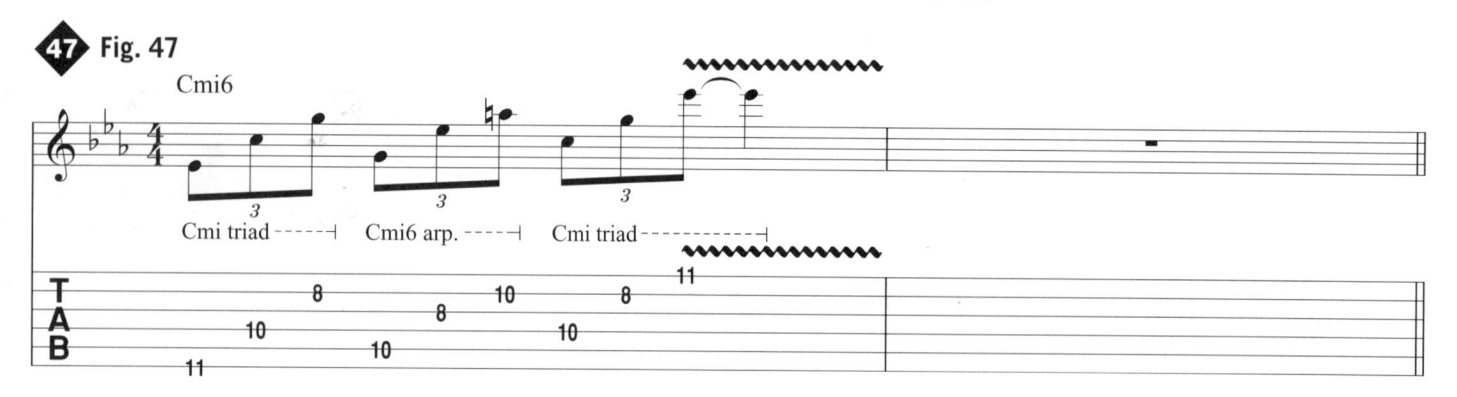

Fig. 47

This tricky move involves shifting an open Ami7♭5 arpeggio up the neck, then ending with an F7 arpeggio.

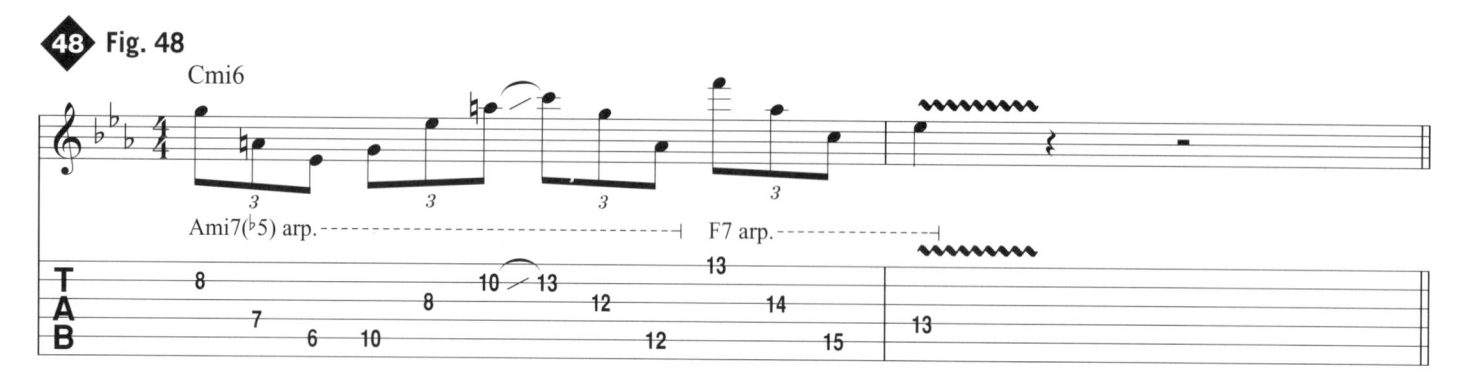

Fig. 48

Fig. 49 slides F triads up the neck, adding the 7th (E♭) and 9th (G) degrees for additional color.

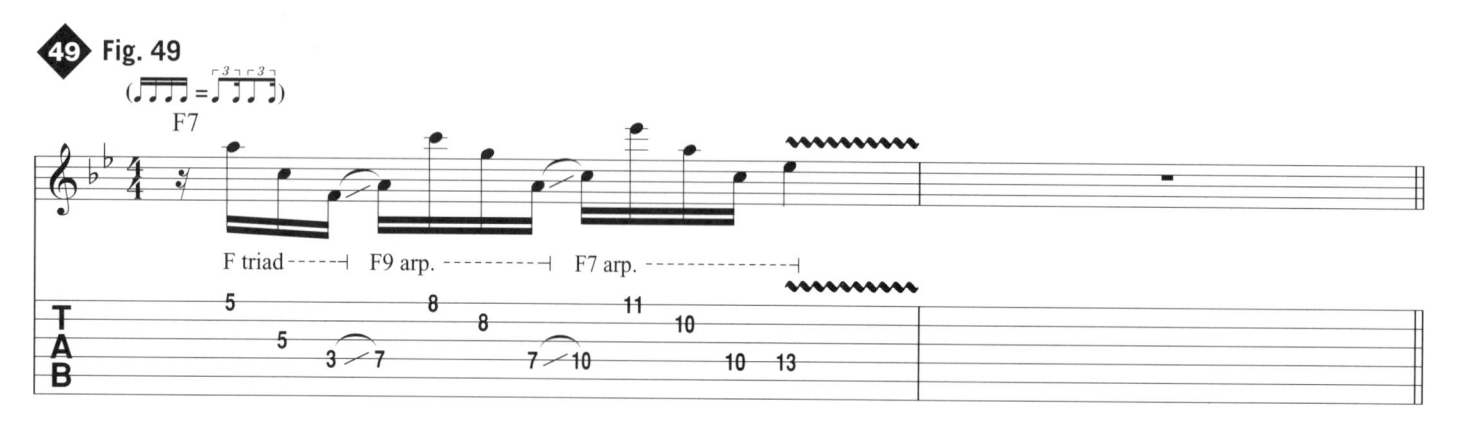

Fig. 49

Fig. 50 begins with a tri-tone substitution (B♭7) on E7♯9, then superimposes C7 and B7 arpeggios for a chromatic descent.

Fig. 50

Acknowledgments

I wish to give special thanks to Marie-Christine Belkadi for maintaining my web site (http://home.earthlink.net/~mcb1), Kevin Holmes for editing assistance, all at Hal Leonard Corporation, Frank Gambale and Mike Stern for their support, Keith Wyatt from Musicians Institution, Steve Blutcher from DiMarzio, HHHrrernst Homeyer for his good advice, Marco Biasella and Pierre Pichon for letting me use their equipment, Alain Lasseube—Le frere Gagarine, Olivier Hermitant for his friendship, and Chris Jero of Yamaha.

This book is dedicated to my dear Grandma, Georgette Bach.

About the Author

Jean-Marc Belkadi started playing guitar at age 14. He graduated from the Toulouse Music Conservatory in his hometown. In 1984, he left France for the U.S. to study at Musicians Institute in Los Angeles where he received the Best Guitarist of the Year award.

In 1989 and 1992, he was awarded third and second prize at the Billboard Song Contest. For three years, he was musical director of the Johnny Hune TV show. He has written three guitar method books—*A Modern Approach to Jazz, Rock, & Fusion Guitar, The Diminished Scale for Guitar,* and *Advanced Scale Concepts and Licks for Guitar*—and has recorded one solo album.

Guitar Notation Legend

Guitar Music can be notated three different ways: on a *musical staff*, in *tablature*, and in *rhythm slashes*.

RHYTHM SLASHES are written above the staff. Strum chords in the rhythm indicated. Use the chord diagrams found at the top of the first page of the transcription for the appropriate chord voicings. Round noteheads indicate single notes.

THE MUSICAL STAFF shows pitches and rhythms and is divided by bar lines into measures. Pitches are named after the first seven letters of the alphabet.

TABLATURE graphically represents the guitar fingerboard. Each horizontal line represents a a string, and each number represents a fret.

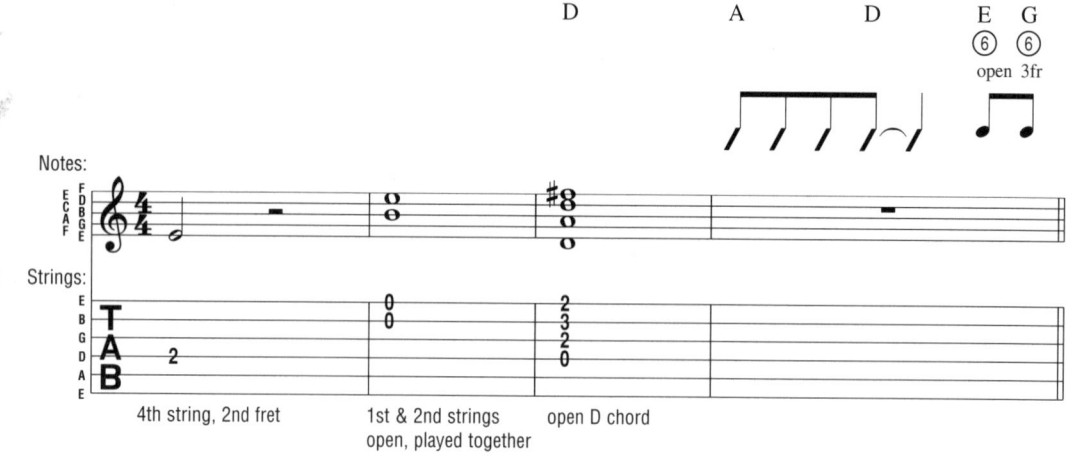

Definitions for Special Guitar Notation

HALF-STEP BEND: Strike the note and bend up 1/2 step.

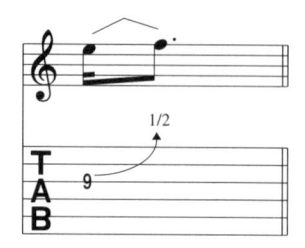

WHOLE-STEP BEND: Strike the note and bend up one step.

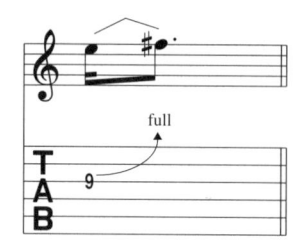

GRACE NOTE BEND: Strike the note and bend up as indicated. The first note does not take up any time.

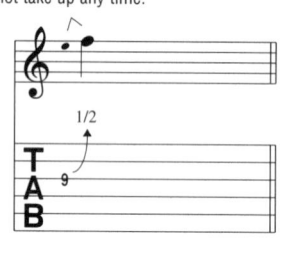

SLIGHT (MICROTONE) BEND: Strike the note and bend up 1/4 step.

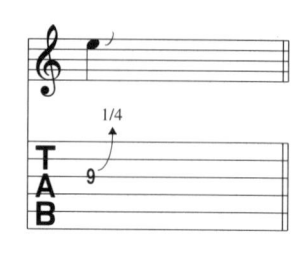

BEND AND RELEASE: Strike the note and bend up as indicated, then release back to the original note. Only the first note is struck.

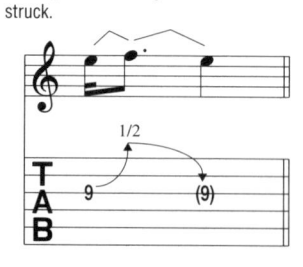

PRE-BEND: Bend the note as indicated, then strike it.

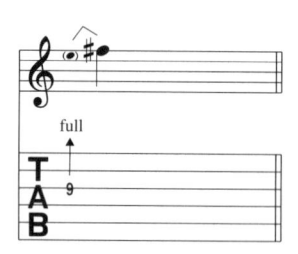

PRE-BEND AND RELEASE: Bend the note as indicated. Strike it and release the bend back to the original note.

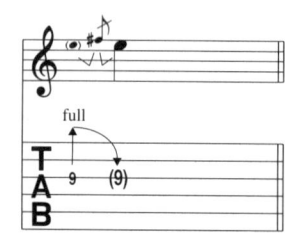

UNISON BEND: Strike the two notes simultaneously and bend the lower note up to the pitch of the higher.

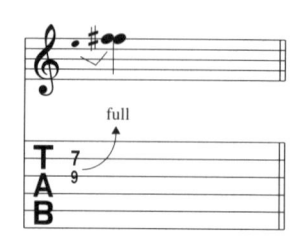

VIBRATO: The string is vibrated by rapidly bending and releasing the note with the fretting hand.

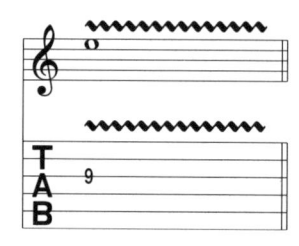

WIDE VIBRATO: The pitch is varied to a greater degree by vibrating with the fretting hand.

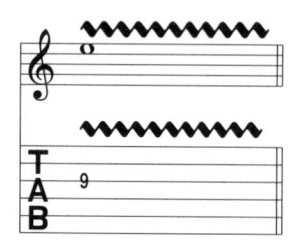

HAMMER-ON: Strike the first (lower) note with one finger, then sound the higher note (on the same string) with another finger by fretting it without picking.

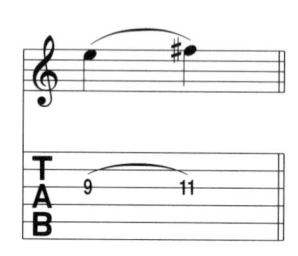

PULL-OFF: Place both fingers on the notes to be sounded. Strike the first note and without picking, pull the finger off to sound the second (lower) note.

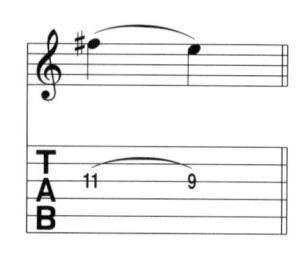

LEGATO SLIDE: Strike the first note and then slide the same fret-hand finger up or down to the second note. The second note is not struck.

SHIFT SLIDE: Same as legato slide, except the second note is struck.

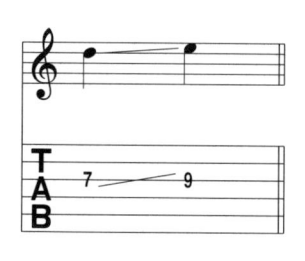

TRILL: Very rapidly alternate between the notes indicated by continuously hammering on and pulling off.

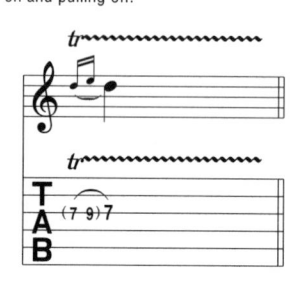

TAPPING: Hammer ("tap") the fret indicated with the pick-hand index or middle finger and pull off to the note fretted by the fret hand.

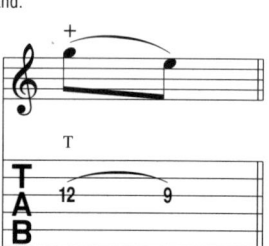

NATURAL HARMONIC: Strike the note while the fret-hand lightly touches the string directly over the fret indicated.

PINCH HARMONIC: The note is fretted normally and a harmonic is produced by adding the edge of the thumb or the tip of the index finger of the pick hand to the normal pick attack.

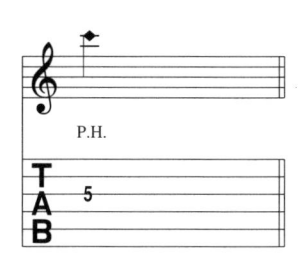

HARP HARMONIC: The note is fretted normally and a harmonic is produced by gently resting the pick hand's index finger directly above the indicated fret (in parentheses) while the pick hand's thumb or pick assists by plucking the appropriate string.

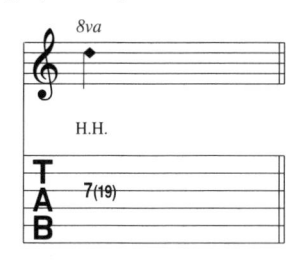

PICK SCRAPE: The edge of the pick is rubbed down (or up) the string, producing a scratchy sound.

MUFFLED STRINGS: A percussive sound is produced by laying the fret hand across the string(s) without depressing, and striking them with the pick hand.

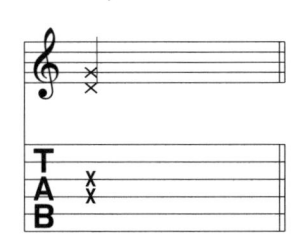

PALM MUTING: The note is partially muted by the pick hand lightly touching the string(s) just before the bridge.

RAKE: Drag the pick across the strings indicated with a single motion.

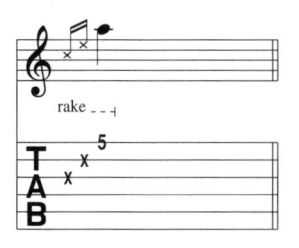

TREMOLO PICKING: The note is picked as rapidly and continuously as possible.

ARPEGGIATE: Play the notes of the chord indicated by quickly rolling them from bottom to top.

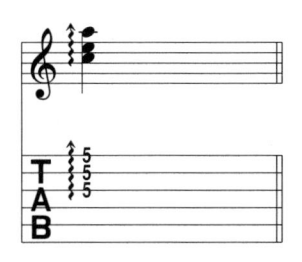

VIBRATO BAR DIVE AND RETURN: The pitch of the note or chord is dropped a specified number of steps (in rhythm) then returned to the original pitch.

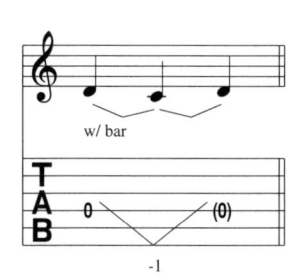

VIBRATO BAR SCOOP: Depress the bar just before striking the note, then quickly release the bar.

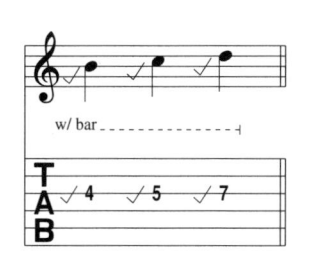

VIBRATO BAR DIP: Strike the note and then immediately drop a specified number of steps, then release back to the original pitch.

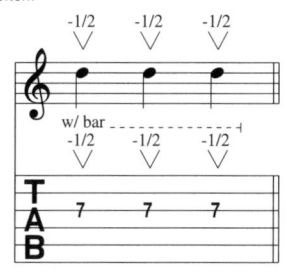

Additional Musical Definitions

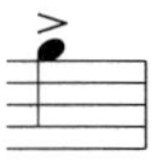

> (accent)	•	Accentuate note (play it louder)
^ (accent)	•	Accentuate note with great intensity
. (staccato)	•	Play the note short
⊓	•	Downstroke
V	•	Upstroke
D.S. al Coda	•	Go back to the sign (𝄋), then play until the measure marked "*To Coda*," then skip to the section labelled "*Coda*."
D.S. al Fine	•	Go back to the beginning of the song and play until the measure marked "*Fine*" (end).

Rhy. Fig.	•	Label used to recall a recurring accompaniment pattern (usually chordal).
Riff	•	Label used to recall composed, melodic lines (usually single notes) which recur.
Fill	•	Label used to identify a brief melodic figure which is to be inserted into the arrangement.
Rhy. Fill	•	A chordal version of a Fill.
tacet	•	Instrument is silent (drops out).
𝄇 𝄆	•	Repeat measures between signs.
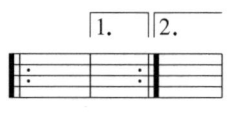 1. 2.	•	When a repeated section has different endings, play the first ending only the first time and the second ending only the second time.

NOTE: Tablature numbers in parentheses mean:
1. The note is being sustained over a system (note in standard notation is tied), or
2. The note is sustained, but a new articulation (such as a hammer-on, pull-off, slide or vibrato begins, or
3. The note is a barely audible "ghost" note (note in standard notation is also in parentheses).

MUSICIANS INSTITUTE Press

Musicians Institute Press

is the official series of Southern California's renowned music school, Musicians Institute. **MI** instructors, some of the finest musicians in the world, share their vast knowledge and experience with you – no matter what your current level. For guitar, bass, drums, vocals, and keyboards, **MI Press** offers the finest music curriculum for higher learning through a variety of series:

ESSENTIAL CONCEPTS
Designed from MI core curriculum programs.

MASTER CLASS
Designed from MI elective courses.

PRIVATE LESSONS
Tackle a variety of topics "one-on-one" with MI faculty instructors.

FOR MORE INFORMATION, SEE YOUR LOCAL MUSIC DEALER, OR WRITE TO:

HAL•LEONARD® CORPORATION
7777 W. BLUEMOUND RD. P.O. BOX 13819 MILWAUKEE, WI 53213

Prices, contents, and availability subject to change without notice. Some products may not be available outside of the U.S.A.

GUITAR

Advanced Scale Concepts & Licks for Guitar
by Jean Marc Belkadi
Private Lessons
00695298 Book/CD Pack $12.95

Basic Blues Guitar
by Steve Trovato
Private Lessons
00695180 Book/CD Pack $12.95

Creative Chord Shapes
by Jamie Findlay
Private Lessons
00695172 Book/CD Pack $7.95

Diminished Scale for Guitar
by Jean Marc Belkadi
Private Lessons
00695227 Book/CD Pack $9.95

Guitar Basics
by Bruce Buckingham
Private Lessons
00695134 Book/CD Pack $14.95

Guitar Hanon
by Peter Deneff
Private Lessons
00695321 .... $9.95

Guitar Soloing
by Dan Gilbert & Beth Marlis
Essential Concepts
00695190 Book/CD Pack $17.95

Harmonics for Guitar
by Jamie Findlay
Private Lessons
00695169 Book/CD Pack $9.95

Jazz Guitar Chord System
by Scott Henderson
Private Lessons
00695291 .... $6.95

Jazz Guitar Improvisation
by Sid Jacobs
Master Class
00695128 Book/CD Pack $17.95

Modern Approach to Jazz, Rock & Fusion Guitar
by Jean Marc Belkadi
Private Lessons
00695143 Book/CD Pack $12.95

Music Reading for Guitar
by David Oakes
Essential Concepts
00695192 .... $16.95

Rhythm Guitar
by Bruce Buckingham & Eric Paschal
Essential Concepts
00695188 .... $16.95

Rock Lead Basics
by Nick Nolan & Danny Gill
Master Class
00695144 Book/CD Pack $14.95

Rock Lead Performance
by Nick Nolan & Danny Gill
Master Class
00695278 Book/CD Pack $16.95

Rock Lead Techniques
by Nick Nolan & Danny Gill
Master Class
00695146 Book/CD Pack $14.95

BASS

Arpeggios for Bass
by Dave Keif
Private Lessons
00695133 .... $12.95

Bass Fretboard Basics
by Paul Farnen
Essential Concepts
00695201 .... $12.95

Bass Playing Techniques
by Alexis Sklarevski
Essential Concepts
00695207 .... $14.95

Grooves for Electric Bass
by David Keif
Private Lessons
00695265 Book/CD Pack $12.95

Music Reading for Bass
by Wendy Wrebovcsik
Essential Concepts
00695203 .... $9.95

Odd-Meter Bassics
by Dino Monoxelos
Private Lessons
00695170 Book/CD Pack $14.95

KEYBOARD

Music Reading for Keyboard
by Larry Steelman
Essential Concepts
00695205 .... $12.95

R & B Soul Keyboard
by Henry J. Brewer
Private Lessons
00695327 .... $16.95

Salsa Hanon
by Peter Deneff
Private Lessons
00695226 .... $10.95

DRUM

Brazilian Coordination for Drumset
by Maria Martinez
Master Class
00695284 Book/CD Pack $14.95

Chart Reading Workbook for Drummers
by Bobby Gabriele
Private Lessons
00695129 Book/CD Pack $14.95

Working the Inner Clock for Drumset
by Phil Maturano
Private Lessons
00695127 Book/CD Pack $16.95

VOICE

Sightsinging
by Mike Campbell
Essential Concepts
00695195 .... $16.95

ALL INSTRUMENTS

An Approach to Jazz Improvisation
by Dave Pozzi
Private Lessons
00695135 Book/CD Pack $17.95

Encyclopedia of Reading Rhythms
by Gary Hess
Private Lessons
00695145 .... $19.95

Going Pro
by Kenny Kerner
Private Lessons
00695322 .... $19.95

Harmony & Theory
by Keith Wyatt & Carl Schroeder
Essential Concepts
00695161 .... $17.95

Lead Sheet Bible
by Robin Randall
Private Lessons
00695130 Book/CD Pack $19.95

WORKSHOP SERIES
Transcribed scores of the greatest songs ever!

Blues Workshop
00695137 .... $19.95

Classic Rock Workshop
00695136 .... $19.95

R & B Workshop
00695138 .... $19.95